## Essential Test Tips Video from Trivium Test Prep!

Dear Customer,

Thank you for purchasing from Trivium Test Prep! We're honored to help you prepare for your OAR exam.

To show our appreciation, we're offering a **FREE OAR Essential Test Tips Video by Trivium Test Prep**.* Our video includes 35 test preparation strategies that will make you successful on the OAR. All we ask is that you email us your feedback and describe your experience with our product. Amazing, awful, or just so-so: we want to hear what you have to say!

To receive your **FREE OAR Essential Test Tips Video**, please email us at 5star@triviumtestprep.com. Include "Free 5 Star" in the subject line and the following information in your email:

1. The title of the product you purchased.

2. Your rating from 1 – 5 (with 5 being the best).

3. Your feedback about the product, including how our materials helped you meet your goals and ways in which we can improve our products.

4. Your full name and shipping address so we can send your **FREE OAR Essential Test Tips Video**.

If you have any questions or concerns please feel free to contact us directly at 5star@triviumtestprep.com.

Thank you!

- Trivium Test Prep Team

*To get access to the free video please email us at 5star@triviumtestprep.com, and please follow the instructions above.

OAR Study Guide:
Officer Aptitude Rating Test
Prep Book with Practice Questions
[5th Edition] [Navy]

Jonathan Cox

Copyright © 2022 by Accepted, Inc.

ISBN-13: 9781637982242

ALL RIGHTS RESERVED. By purchase of this book, you have been licensed one copy for personal use only. No part of this work may be reproduced, redistributed, or used in any form or by any means without prior written permission of the publisher and copyright owner. Accepted, Inc.; Trivium Test Prep; Cirrus Test Prep; and Ascencia Test Prep are all imprints of Trivium Test Prep, LLC.

NMOTC was not involved in the creation or production of this product, is not in any way affiliated with Accepted, Inc., and does not sponsor or endorse this product. All test names (or their acronyms) are trademarks of their respective owners. This study guide is for general information and does not claim endorsement by any third party.

Questions regarding permissions or copyrighting may be sent to support@acceptedinc.com.

Image(s) used under license from Shutterstock.com

# Table of Contents

1. Introduction ............................................................................................................................. 1
   1.1 – Sections on the OAR ..................................................................................................... 1
   1.2 – Additional Test Information ......................................................................................... 1
2. Mathematics Knowledge ........................................................................................................ 2
   2.1 – Introduction .................................................................................................................. 2
   2.2 – Study Information ........................................................................................................ 2
      2.2.1 – Number Theory ..................................................................................................... 2
      2.2.2 – Working with Fractions ......................................................................................... 9
      2.2.3 – Algebra ................................................................................................................ 12
      2.2.4 – Geometry ............................................................................................................ 15
   2.3 – Tips .............................................................................................................................. 20
   2.4 – Practice Questions ...................................................................................................... 22
   2.4.1 – Practice Questions Answer Key ............................................................................... 25
      2.5 – Review and Takeaways ........................................................................................... 26
      2.5.1 – Review .................................................................................................................. 26
      2.5.2 – Takeaways ............................................................................................................ 26
3. Paragraph Comprehension .................................................................................................... 27
   3.1 – Introduction ................................................................................................................ 27
   3.2 – Study Information ...................................................................................................... 32
      3.2.1 – Main Ideas ........................................................................................................... 33
      3.2.2 – Drawing Conclusions ........................................................................................... 34
      3.2.3 – Stated Facts ......................................................................................................... 35
      3.2.4 – Mood and Tone ................................................................................................... 36
      3.2.5 – Purpose ............................................................................................................... 36
      3.2.6 – Technique ............................................................................................................ 37
      3.2.7 – Sequence of Events ............................................................................................. 39
      3.2.8 – Reworded Facts ................................................................................................... 39

3.3 – Tips ............................................................................................................. 40

3.4 – Practice Questions ..................................................................................... 42

3.4.1 – Practice Questions Answer Key ............................................................... 46

    3.5 – Review and Takeaways ........................................................................... 47

    3.5.1 – Review ................................................................................................. 47

    3.5.2 – Takeaways ........................................................................................... 47

4. Mechanical Comprehension ................................................................................ 48

4.1 – Introduction ................................................................................................ 48

4.2 – Study Information ...................................................................................... 48

    4.2.1 – Materials .............................................................................................. 48

    4.2.2 – Structural Support ................................................................................ 49

    4.2.3 – Fluid Dynamics .................................................................................... 50

    4.2.4 – Mechanical Motion .............................................................................. 51

    4.2.5 – Simple Machines ................................................................................. 53

    4.2.6 – Compound Machines .......................................................................... 58

4.3 – Tips ............................................................................................................. 61

4.4 – Practice Questions ..................................................................................... 63

4.4.1 – Practice Questions Answer Key ............................................................... 66

    4.5 – Review and Takeaways ........................................................................... 67

    4.5.1 – Review ................................................................................................. 67

    4.5.2 – Takeaways ........................................................................................... 67

5. OAR Practice Test #1 .......................................................................................... 69

    5.1 – OAR Practice Test #1 Answer Key ........................................................... 91

6. OAR Practice Test #2 .......................................................................................... 94

    6.1 – OAR Practice Test #2 Answer Key ......................................................... 118

Exclusive Test Tips .................................................................................................. 121

7. Conclusion ........................................................................................................ 1219

# 1. Introduction

If you plan on going to the Navy Officer Candidate School, you will need to take either the OAR exam (Officer Aptitude Rating), or alternatively may take the ASTB-E if you want to be a flight officer. Either way, you do NOT need to take both as the ASTB-E comprises all sections of the OAR, but just adds in a couple extra test areas. The concepts tested on the OAR exam are as follows: Math Skills, Reading Comprehension, and Mechanical Comprehension.

## 1.1 – Sections on the OAR

There are 3 sections on the OAR as follows:
1. Math Skills Test (MST) – 30 questions, 40 minutes
2. Reading Comprehension Test (RCT) – 20 questions, 30 minutes
3. Mechanical Comprehension Test (MCT) – 30 questions, 15 minutes

## 1.2 – Additional Test Information

Be sure that you visit www.med.navy.mil/sites/nmotc/nami/pages/astboverview.aspx or simply Google "ASTB" (OAR is a 3 of the 7 sections found on the ASTB Exam) and it will be the very first result, and review all the information on that page. This is the official source for information regarding the ASTB as well as the OAR exam, so it is highly important you familiarize yourself with the content on that page and other sections of the website as well.

# 2. Mathematics Knowledge

## 2.1 – Introduction

The purpose of this section on the test is to make sure you fully understand the concepts which are important in high school mathematics courses. This includes information about basic operations, the order operations need to be done in, geometry, and algebra. It also includes working with fractions, which can prove difficult for many people.

## 2.2 – Study Information

### 2.2.1 – Number Theory

The very first thing that you need to understand when you are looking at number theory is the concept of whole numbers. These are going to, generally, be the numbers that you use to count. Thus, 10, 9, 8, 7, 6… will all be considered whole numbers. Number theory is the study of the properties of whole numbers and a whole other set of numbers which are called integers, which consists of all numbers which can be written without the use of a fractional part. The set of integers will include the following:

- Whole numbers
- Negative numbers
- Zero

The natural numbers or whole numbers, do not include negative numbers (or the inverses of the whole numbers).

**Prime Numbers**

Prime numbers are numbers which have only two factors, 1 and itself. Examples would include 5, 7, 11, 13, 19, and 23, among many others. Any number without additional factors is going to be considered a prime number. When you are attempting to figure out if a number is a prime number or not, all you need to do is figure out whether other numbers, besides 1 and the number itself, will divide evenly into it.

Here are a couple of examples:

>Is 66 a prime number?

66 is not going to be considered a prime number. It can be divided as 2 and 33, as 11 and 6, or as 1 and 66.

>Is 21 a prime number?

No. 7 and 3 will divide into it in addition to 1 and 21.

It is important to note that prime numbers are usually going to be odd, with the exception of the number 2. Even numbers, clearly can be divided by 2, so it won't work for larger numbers.

## Multiples

Multiples of numbers are what results from multiplying whole numbers by another factor of that whole numbers. This would be, for instance, any number that has a factor of 7 being multiplied by any other number that has a factor of 7.

Common multiples of two numbers are the numbers which are multiples of both. If you were looking at, say, 4 and 8, then 2 would be a common multiple. 4 would also be a common multiple of the two numbers.

The least common multiple the smallest common multiple that two given numbers share. The fastest way to find this is to just write out the first few multiples for both numbers that you have available and then figure out which one is the smallest. This is not a particularly difficult task, but you will have to understand how multiples work in order to do it properly.

## Exponents

Exponents and exponential notation are utilized to help simply expressions, particularly when factors are repeated multiple times. Exponents are written as superscripts above the number that has the exponent. For example:

$$8 \times 8 = 8^2$$

Both of the above mean the same thing. In all, exponents are actually just a shorthand which is used to help keep the math straight and stop it from becoming too confusing. This can be seen below:

$$5 \times 5 \times 5 \times 5 \times 5 \times 5 = 5^6$$

As you can see, writing the number as an exponent makes it much easier to see what is happening and, ultimately, will simplify equations for you. Another way to say, in words, what is happening above would be to say that it is "five to the sixth power" or "five to the sixth". To see how this might look if you were writing it in an equation, look at the following:

$$2 + 2 \times 5 \times 5 \times 6 \times 7 + 8 = 2 + 2 \times 5^2 \times 6 \times 7 + 8$$

Does it simplify that equation a lot? Not in this case, but it does make it a little bit simpler to read.

## Factoring

When you multiply two numbers together and the result is another whole number, you have found a factor. The complete list of factors for any given whole number is going to be the set of each number that can be multiplied to reach the number. Here is an example:

What are the factors which can be used to reach 24?

1 and 24, 2 and 12, 3 and 8, 6 and 4

It is not necessary to write them like that, but it will help you keep them in mind if you keep the factors together with their counterparts.

If you want to figure out whether a number is a factor of another one or not, just divide the number by the potential factor and see if the result is a whole number. Every number will have at least two factors, 1 and the number itself. So the two factors of, say, 2 are 1 and 2.

## Common Divisors

Numbers which are the factors of more than one whole number are known as common factors. For instance, 6 would be a common factor of both 12 and 24 (because it can be multiplied by 2 to reach 12 and 4 to reach 24).

## Square Roots

The term "square root" is used to describe a number which can be squared to equal the number provided.

Radical forms are used to show square roots in equations, even if they are not going to be even or easy to calculate. The symbol which is typically utilized for a square root is $\sqrt{}$.

Some numbers will have very clean whole numbers for their roots. These are known as perfect squares. Here is a table which shows common perfect squares:

| Number | Perfect Square | Square Root |
|--------|----------------|-------------|
| 1      | 1              | $\sqrt{1}$  |
| 2      | 4              | $\sqrt{4}$  |
| 3      | 9              | $\sqrt{9}$  |
| 4      | 16             | $\sqrt{16}$ |
| 5      | 25             | $\sqrt{25}$ |
| 6      | 36             | $\sqrt{36}$ |
| 7      | 49             | $\sqrt{49}$ |
| 8      | 64             | $\sqrt{64}$ |
| 9      | 81             | $\sqrt{81}$ |
| 10     | 100            | $\sqrt{100}$|

## Order of Operations

The order of operations is, perhaps obviously, the way that the operations need to be done in order to reach the correct answer. Some operations will take precedence over others and, thus, the operations need to be done in a specific order.

Here is the basic order of operations:

1. First take care of any operations which are within a grouping symbol such as parentheses () or brackets [].
2. Next handle the roots and the exponents.
3. Net handle the multiplication and division in the same order that they appear (left to right).
4. Finally, handle the addition and subtraction (again, moving from left to right).

For an example of why this is important, consider the following:

Solve: 2 + 2 x 2

If you ignore the order of operations, what do you get?

2 + 2 = 4 x 2 = 8

Now if you were to follow the order of operations, what happens?

2 x 2 = 4 + 2 = 6

Two different answers. It will always be like this when problems are being done. It is important to eliminate any ambiguous statements in equations, because precision is key. That is why the order of operations is very important.

There is an acronym which can be used to help you remember the order of operations:

PEMDAS

Parentheses, Exponents, Multiplication, Division, Addition, Subtraction

If you are using PEMDAS, you need to remember that multiplication and division as well as addition and subtraction are really one single step, respectively.

## Working with Integers

Integers is a set that includes all whole numbers and the negatives of those numbers as well. For example:

$$...-3, -2, -1, 0, 1, 2, 3...$$

The issue that is at the core here, and perhaps the entire point, is that you can be asked to work with negative numbers in addition to positive numbers. One of the best ways to wrap your head around this is to think about subtraction in general as *adding negative numbers* and think about adding negative numbers as *subtracting positive numbers*. All three operations are, ultimately, the same thing.

$$4 - 4 = 4 + -4$$

## Addition and Subtraction with Positives and Negatives

At its core, there are two situations you will encounter when you have to add integers. Are the numbers the same sign or are the numbers opposite signs? If the numbers are the same, then you can just add them or subtract them like you normally would. Here are a few example situations:

$$3 + 3 = 6$$

$$-3 + -3 = -6$$

So how do you handle a situation when the two numbers have different signs? Easy, ignore the signs, and then subtract the smaller from the larger, then utilize the exact same sign that the larger of the two has. Here are a few examples:

$$3 + -4 = -1$$

$$-5 + 4 = 1$$

Subtraction is the same way...with one small difference. Two negatives make a positive, right? So consider the following:

$$2 - -2 = 2 + 2 = 4$$

In all, the best way to handle subtraction with negative numbers is to just turn the problem into an addition problem.

## **Multiplication and Division with Positives and Negatives**

Again, the best way to handle this is to ignore the signs and then multiply or divide like you normally would. To figure out what sign the final product will have, you simply have to figure out how many negatives are in the numbers you worked with. If the number of negatives is even, the result will be a positive number. If the number of negatives is odd, the result will be a negative numbers.

For example:

$$2 \times 2 \times -2 = -8$$

$$-2 \times -2 \times 2 = 8$$

$$-2 \times -2 \times -2 = -8$$

## **Exponents of Negative Numbers**

Exponents with negative numbers are simple: If the number with the exponent is negative and the exponent is even, the result will be positive. If the number with the exponent is negative and the exponent is odd, the result will be negative.

For example:

$$-4^4 = 256$$

$$-4^3 = -64$$

The reason for this is simple, even for the two examples above:

$$-4 \times -4 \times -4 \times -4 = 256$$

$$-4 \times -4 \times -4 = -64$$

You have to remember that exponents are just another way of writing out multiplication.

## 2.2.2 – Working with Fractions

Check the arithmetic review section of this guide for information on how to convert fractions back and forth. This section will cover different types of fractions and how to perform operations on that fraction.

**Equivalent Fractions**

One of the most common things that you will do when you are working with fractions is to simplify them. Another way to state this is to "reduce" fractions. All this means is writing the fraction in the smallest equivalent fraction you can (as in – with the smallest numbers). (5/10) would be simplified as (1/2). (2/4) could also be simplified as (1/2).

Here are some things to keep in mind when you are trying to simplify fractions:

- You need to find a number that can evenly divide into the bottom and the top number of the fraction that you are simplifying. After that, you can do the actual division.
- Once the division is finished, check to make sure your fraction cannot be further simplified. It is easy to make this mistake and even if you do it and find an equivalent fraction, the fraction will not be fully simplified and the question will be marked wrong.
- You can use simplification to reduce fractions to lower terms by dividing the top and bottom by the same number. You can also, perhaps more important, raise fractions to higher terms if you multiply both the top and the bottom numbers by the same number. This is very important in the addition and subtraction of fractions.

Here is an example of reducing a fraction:

$$6/9 = 2/3$$

The largest number you can divide into both of the numbers in the fraction (6 and 9) is 3. 6/3 = 2 and 9/3 = 3, giving the new fraction: 2/3.

Here is an example of raising a fraction:

$$2/4 = 4/8$$

Simply multiply the 2 and the 4 each by 2 and you get the new equivalent fraction: 4/8.

## Addition and Subtraction

To add and subtract fractions, you need to understand two terms:

- **Denominator** – The number on the bottom of a fraction.
- **Numerator** – The number on the top of a fraction.

If you have two numbers which have the same denominator, then you will have what is known as a common denominator. You can really only add or subtract fractions that have a common denominator, so if you do not have one, you need to make one.

Here are the steps for adding and subtracting fractions:

1. If the fractions have a common denominator, then proceed as usual. If not, then reduce or raise one or both fractions until you have a common denominator.
2. Add or subtract the numerators as you would any number, ignoring the denominator.
3. Place the resulting sum (or difference) on top of the common denominator as the new numerator.
4. Simplify the new fraction as much as possible.

Step 1 is involved with coming up with what is known as the least common denominator. This is the smallest number that all fractions in question can have as a common denominator. The process of doing this is the same as the process for finding the least common multiple.

Remember that you can turn mixed numbers into improper fractions. This is useful for addition, but it is not always necessary, for instance:

$$2 ½ + 3 ¾ = (5/2) + (15/4) = 2 + 3 + ½ + ¾$$

The last part of this provides something interesting: You can simply add the whole number parts, then add the fractional parts, then add the two together. This will save you a lot of trouble and extra steps. It is just as correct as any other method of solving the problem and, of course, remember that you are not being tested on how you did it, just that it was done.

## Multiplication and Division

The multiplication and division of fractions is actually simpler than adding or subtracting them. When you have to multiply fractions together, all you have to do is multiply the numerators to get the new numerator and then multiply the denominators to get the new denominator. Once that is done, you can go ahead and simplify.

For example:

$$(2/5) \times (3/7) =$$

$$2 \times 3 = 6$$

$$5 \times 7 = 35$$

$$6/35$$

There you have the new fraction: 6/35. There is no way to simplify it, so it stands on its own as the answer.

Division is a little bit more complicated, but ultimately it is the same procedure. First, you have to find the reciprocal of the second fraction. A reciprocal is a fraction which has its numerator and denominator switched. Once that is done, you will multiply the fractions as usual.

Here is an example:

$$(5/6) \div (2/3) =$$

$$(5/6) \times (3/2) =$$

$$5 \times 3 = 15$$

$$6 \times 2 = 12$$

$$15/12$$

$$5/4$$

As you can see, the second fraction (2/3) simply flips to (3/2). The common way this is explained is to "flip and multiply". That is as good an explanation as any, and is certainly easier to remember than the way that uses all of the terminologies. Again, you are being tested on your ability to do the math here, not to know the jargon.

## 2.2.3 – Algebra

Algebra is a method of generalizing expressions involved in arithmetic. You will be able to explain how groups of things are handled all the time. This is useful for times when you have a certain function that you need to do over and over again. In algebra, you have a few different types of numbers in addition to symbols which can be used to stand for certain numbers. There are also a variety of techniques which can be used to help explain how these are solved. Typically, you will start using algebra initially when you are attempting to work with word problems. You will also see it creep in with a bunch of the equations used in this guide to explain complex subtest concepts.

### Evaluating Numbers

Numbers which are assigned a definite value are constants. For instance: 1 is always 1, 2 is always 2, $\pi$ is always $\pi$. There are a number of others that you will become aware of the more you work. When symbols are used to stand for numbers, they can typically take on any number. If you saw the equation: $2x = 4$, x would be the variable here.

A few things to keep in mind:

- You can make a variable anything you want. X, y, Z, a, A, b, etc.
- Both sides of the = sign are, obviously, =. This is how you solve equations.
- Once you have figured out what a variable is, plug it into the original equation to make sure everything is still equal.

### Equations

Equations are expressions that have an equal sign, such as $2 + 2 = 4$. Equations will usually have a variable, and will always be true or false. $2 + 2 = 1$ is false. $2 + 2 = 4$ is true. When you are solving for variables, only one answer for each variable, usually, will make the expression true. That is the number you must find.

Basically, to do this, you will just rewrite the equation in more and more simple terms until you have the solution to it. Ideally, you want this to be x (or whatever variable) = a number.

$$x = \#$$

You can do anything to an equation as long as you do the same thing to both sides. This is how you solve equations.

Here is an example showing this:

$$3x - 7 = -7 + 9$$

First, add 7 to both sides:

$$3x - 7 + 7 = -7 + 9 + 7$$

$$3x = 9$$

That gets rid of the 7s. Now, simplify this by dividing both sides of the equation by 3. Note: You have to divide the *entire* side by 3, not just one part of it:

$$(3x)/3 = 9/3$$

$$x = 3$$

The solution is now solved.


**Word Problems**


Word problems often utilize algebraic principles in their text. It is important to know how to properly assign a variable inside of a word problem. Pay attention to the words used: "x equals", "x is less than", "2 is added to x", so on and so forth. That is the part you need to pay the closest attention to when going through these problems.

If you are not given a specific variable but you need one, just call it whatever you want. "x" is the simplest variable you can use to do this, and is also one of the least confusing when you start working with more complex algebraic principles.

## Exponents – Multiplication

Multiplying variables with exponents is simple. Just add the exponents together to get the new exponent. Keep in mind how exponents work as well, that is important.

Here is an example of exponents with variables:

$$x * x * x = x^3$$

Here is an example showing the multiplication of exponents:

$$x^2 * x^3 = x^5$$

## Factoring

Factoring is the process of breaking one quantity down into the product of some other quantity (or quantities). When you learned to use distribution to multiply out variables, you are learning to do the opposite of factoring. When you factor, you are removing parts of an equation in order to turn it into factors. Basically, you do this by removing the single largest common single figure (monomial) factor.

Here is an example of this in action:

$$\text{Factor the following: } 3x^2 - 9x$$

Basically, you will pull out the largest common denominator between the two of them. In this case, it is 3x. So you will be left with the following:

$$3x(x - 3)$$

It is also possible to do this with expressions that have more than two figures. Usually, these will be trinomials, with 3 terms. These will always end up being in the form of (x )(x ). What the second number is and what the sign is for the problem is determined by the original problem.

## Simplification

You can simplify algebraic expressions the exact same way that you would fractions. Basically, you cake out the common factors. They just cancel out. You will want to multiply everything out if you cannot find a factor and then simplify.

Here is an example

$$[2(x + 4)]/[x + 4]$$

$$(x + 4)(x + 4) / (x + 4)$$

$$x + 4$$

Make sense? Of course, it gets more complicated than that, but this is the simplest way to handle the method of taking care of these problems.

### 2.2.4 – Geometry

The geometry section here is pretty straightforward. See the arithmetic reasoning portion of the guide for an extensive look at both squares and rectangles. New information will be covered here.

## Angles

Angles are measured in degrees. Just as an example, if you were to completely rotate around a circle a single time, you would have gone 360 degrees. Half is 180 degrees. A quarter is 90 degrees, and so on. Degrees are used to talk about what fraction of a total rotation around a circle a certain angle represents.

Here is some terminology to keep in mind:

- **Acute angles** – Angles with a measurement of fewer than 90 degrees.
- **Right angles** – Angles with a measurement of exactly 90 degrees.
- **Obtuse angles** – Angles with a measurement of more than 90 degrees.

- **Complementary angles** – Two angles which add up to 90 degrees.
- **Supplementary angles** – Two angles which add up to 180 degrees.

## Triangles

Triangles are geometric figures that have three sides (which are straight). The most important thing you need to know about triangles is that the sum of the measurements of the angles is always going to equal 180. This is important because it means that if you know two of them, you can very easily calculate the third simply by subtracting the first two from 180. There are three types of triangles that you need to know about:

- **Equilateral triangles** – These are triangles in which the three angles are the same measure. Each one of the angles is 60 degrees.
- **Isosceles triangles** – These are triangles which have two sides of the same length. The two angles which are directly opposite the sides of the same length will be the same angle. If B was the third angle, then you could state that lines between A and B (AB) and between lines B and C (BC) are the same. AB = BC.
- **Right triangles** – These might be the most important. A right triangle is a triangle which has one side that equals 90 degrees. Two sides are legs and the third side, which is directly opposite the 90-degree angle, is the hypotenuse, the longest one of the sides.

With right triangles, you can always remember that the lengths of the sides are related by the following equation (the Pythagorean Theorem, for those of you who remember):

$$a^2 + b^2 = c^2$$

Where $c$ is the hypotenuse, the side which is opposite the right angle. It is the longest of the sides.

## Circles

Circles, as you probably are already aware, are closed lines. In a circle, every single point is going to be the exact same distance from the center of the circle (or, more accurately, from a fixed point located at the center of the circle. If you draw a line from the outside of the circle to the fixed point in the center, you have the radius. If you draw a line from one side of the circle straight through to the other, passing through the center point, you have the diameter.

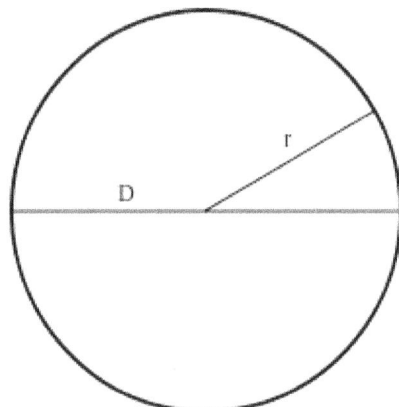

For a circle, remember:

diameter = 2radius

You can use the radius to find out the circumference of a circle (how big it is around), by using the following formula:

$C$ = circumference

$r$ = radius

$$C = 2\pi r$$

Think of the circumference like the perimeter of the circle.

To find the area of a circle, use the following formula:

$A$ = area

$r$ = radius

$$A = \pi r^2$$

## The Coordinate System

The coordinate system or, sometimes, the Cartesian coordinate system, is a method of locating and describing points on a two-dimensional plane. It is, at its core, a reference system. The plant is two number lines which have been laid out perpendicular to each other, with the point that they cross being the 0 point for both lines. Positive and negative integers are both represented in this system.

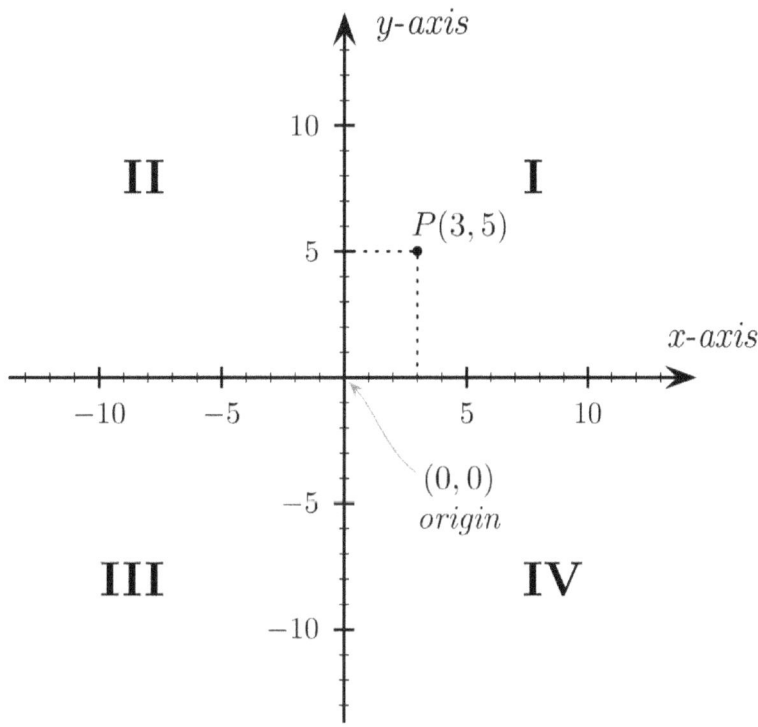

In the image above, each small tick on the line is equal to one. The larger ticks represent multiples of 5. A point is also depicted, P, which shows how things are placed onto the coordinate system. The horizontal line on the coordinate plane is called the x-axis. The vertical line on the coordinate plane called the y-axis. The points, when described, are described in reference to where they lie on that plane.

Here is an example:

(2, 3)

The first number, 2, is the x-axis. The second, 3, is the y-axis. So this point is at position 2 of the x-axis and position 3 of the y-axis.

A way to simplify the way these points work is to say:

$$(x, y)$$

## **Slope**

The slope is the steepness of a given line. When you look on the coordinate plane, if you draw a line between two points, you will get the slope. The slope has a variety of uses, but for now, you just need to understand what the slope actually is.

Here is the way to find slope:

Point A: $(x_1, y_1)$

Point B: $(x_2, y_2)$

$$\text{Slope} = (y_2 - y_1)/(x_2 - x_1)$$

In plain English, you will take the difference between the y coordinates and divide them by the difference between the x coordinates. Remember: y is vertical and x is horizontal.

Here is an example of how this type of problem would likely manifest:

Find the slope of a line with that goes through the following points: (9, 3), (2, 12)

First, set the problem up:

$$(12-3) / (2-9)$$

Next, solve the differences:

$$9 / -7$$

That is the slope. 9/-7. You can solve this for a decimal, but there is no need to do that. Slopes are, inherently, measures of steepness that can be used on the coordinate plane. To take it further would be to remove the usefulness of the value itself.

## 2.3 – Tips

Here are some tips to help you make it through the mathematics knowledge section of the OAR:

- Remember to utilize PEMDAS and the order of operations when you are working through problems.
- Practice makes perfect. You know the types of questions that are going to be asked here, the only thing you need to do is make sure that you are able to solve them.
- Be careful with the answers. The test will often provide red herrings for common mistakes that you might make in the form of correct answers for the wrong problems.
- Since you will not have access to a calculator, you will need to round π. 3.14 is the most common way to do this. Sometimes you may be asked to simply include it in your answer without actually utilizing the digits in your calculations at all.
- Don't mix up the perimeter and area formulas.
- One way to get good at algebra relatively quickly is to set up all of your problems, even simple ones, as algebra problems. Remember, you can simply create a variable and stick it on one side of the equation to solve for it. 10 + 10 becomes 10 + 10 = x. So on and so forth.
- Keep in mind that, unlike many tests you probably remember taking in high school, you are not being tested on your ability to write out how you solved the problem. There are many correct ways to solve mathematical problems and, as long as you come to the right answer in the end, it does not matter how you solved it. Nobody will be coming behind you and checking your scratch paper to see what you did (unless they think you are cheating, but that is a whole other ball of wax).
- Pay close attention to the positive and negative signs in the work that you are doing. This is extremely important because, again, they will likely throw the correct answers out there as one of the choices but with the wrong sign.
- Always make sure the fractions that you are working with are simplified when you finish with them. Unless otherwise stated, the test answers will usually want the most simplified version of the fraction.
- Make sure you go step by step through each question. Don't skip steps or combine steps. Doing either could lead to an issue where something is accidentally missed.

- It might help you to change even the normal expressions into algebra. Often, understanding what you are being asked to do and knowing how to handle certain problems is only made easier when you are using algebra to handle it.

## 2.4 – Practice Questions

1. Evaluate the expression 4x/(x-1) when x=5.
    a. 3
    b. 4
    c. 5
    d. 6

2. Simplify: 3x^3+4x-(2x+5y)+y
    a. 3x^3+2x+y
    b. 11x-4y
    c. 3x^3+2x-4y
    d. 29x-4y

3. Simplify: (x + 7)(x – 5)
    a. $x^2$ + 2x – 35
    b. $x_2$ + 2x - 35
    c. 35x
    d. 7x + 5x – 35

4. Simplify the expression (4xy)^3/(x^5 y).
    a. 12/x^4
    b. 12 ⟦x^2 y⟧ ^2
    c. 64 ⟦x^2 y⟧ ^2
    d. (64y^2)/x^2

5. Find the area of a rectangular athletic field that is 100 meters long and 45 meters wide.
    a. 290 meters
    b. 4,500 $m^2$
    c. 145 $m^2$
    d. 4.5 $km^2$

6. 2 identical circles are drawn next to each other with their sides just touching; both circles are enclosed in a rectangle whose sides are tangent to the circles. If each circle's radius is 2 inches, find the area of the rectangle.
    a. 24 $cm^2$
    b. 8 $cm^2$
    c. 32 $cm^2$
    d. 16 $cm^2$

7. Mary runs 3 miles north, 4 miles east, 5 miles south, and 2 miles west. What are her final coordinates (in miles), with respect to her starting point?
    a. (8,6)
    b. (-2,6)
    c. (7,3)
    d. (2,-2)

8. Solve for $a$: $3a + 4 = 2a$
    a. $a = -4$
    b. $a = 4$
    c. $a = \frac{-4}{5}$
    d. $a = \frac{4}{5}$

9. Evaluate the expression $|3x - y| + |2y - x|$ if $x = -4$ and $y = -1$.
    a. $-11$
    b. $11$
    c. $13$
    d. $-13$

10. Solve for $x$: $8x - 6 = 3x + 24$
    a. $x = 3.6$
    b. $x = 5$
    c. $x = 6$
    d. $x = 2.5$

11. Convert 0.25 into a percentage
    a. 250%
    b. 2.5%
    c. 25%
    d. 0.25%

12. -2x + -3x² + 4x =
    a. -3x² − 2x
    b. -3x² + 2x
    c. 3x² + 2x
    d. 3x² − 2x

13. Convert 38/98 into a percentage. Round to the nearest percent.
    a. 38%
    b. 38.7%
    c. 38.77%
    d. 38.775%

14. Factor the following: $x^2 + 4x + 4$
    a. $2(x + 2)(x + 2)$
    b. $(x - 2)(x - 2)$
    c. $(x - 2)(x + 2)$
    d. $(x + 2)(x + 2)$

15. Solve for $x$: $4x + 3 > -9$
    a. $x < 3$
    b. $x > -3$
    c. $x > -1\frac{1}{2}$
    d. $x < 1\frac{1}{2}$

**2.4.1 – Practice Questions Answer Key**

1. C.
2. C.
3. A.
4. D.
5. B.
6. C.
7. D.
8. A.
9. C.
10. C.
11. C.
12. B.
13. A.
14. D.
15. B.

## 2.5 – Review and Takeaways

This is a relatively straightforward section. It is meant to test your ability to complete basic high school level mathematical operations.

### 2.5.1 – Review

- **Number theory** – All about numbers. The basics, the order of operations, different operations, different number systems.
- **Fractions** – How to handle fractions. Working with them in terms of operations, manipulating them, and converting them to percentages and decimals.
- **Algebra** – An overview of basic algebra, using variables, and problems you might encounter when dealing with it.
- **Geometry** – Shapes. Circles, squares, triangles, etc. What they are, how they are used, perimeters, areas, etc. This also includes things like slope and the coordinate plane.

### 2.5.2 – Takeaways

The most important thing to take away from this section is that practice makes perfect. If you do a quick online search, you will find thousands of examples and practice problems to help you get through this section. Start working on them in your free time. One thing you could do to assist yourself in this is to just make up problems and equations when you get a free minute and then solve them on your own.

# 3. Paragraph Comprehension

## 3.1 – Introduction

The purpose of the paragraph comprehension section of the OAR is to figure out how well you understand the things that you read. It also measures the level of your ability to retain information that you have read in passages. This is one of the 4 subtests on the OAR which has its score counted toward your AFQB score, so scoring a high number on this subtest is important to your future military career. There are 15 questions on this test which are based on either 15 distinct passages or a number of passages less than 15. Each passage will have a set of questions that is associated with it and you will generally have to pick the answer that best answers a question or fills in a statement to make it complete.

There are two skills which are used to help you understand the things that you read. One of them is the ability to understand what the passage you have read actually says. This is the literal reading of the passage. Some of the questions found on the test are going to ask you to determine what a passage means or to paraphrase something which has been said. To understand a paraphrase, you will have to understand what the original passage means, obviously. This also means you need to understand words in the context of the passage. Vocabulary will help with this.

The second skill you need is the ability to analyze the things that you read. This means you will have to go a bit deeper than the literal interpretation of the passage. You will be asked, at times, to draw conclusions based on information contained within the passage itself. This will often require you to figure out things which are stated indirectly (or not at all) in the content of the passage. Sometimes you will be asked about the tone of the passage or the mood that it evokes.

There are a few types of questions that you will likely encounter in this section of the test:

**Main Idea Questions**

This type of question wants you to give a general statement about what the paragraph you have read means.

Here is an example of this type of question:

> *The economy is making a slow comeback. The housing boom of the 90s is not back, but it should be clear that the economy is improving from where it was just a few years ago. This is even in the face of fruit markets which have been slowing down, causing trouble for bankers and others as well.*

> What is the main idea of the prompt listed above?
>
> A – The economy is not doing well.
>
> B – The economy is on its way back.
>
> C – Bankers are losing money.
>
> D – The apple market isn't good.

The answer here is B. The thesis statement in the first sentence says the economy is on an upswing. Bankers may be losing money, the apply market (and other fruit markets) may not be doing well, but the economy in general is improving, making B the best choice in this situation.

**Sequence of Events Questions**

These types of questions are asking about the order that events occur in the passage.

Here is an example of a sequence of events type of question:

> *The walls were the first thing to fall. Once they had fallen, ranks quickly began to break and the soldiers prepared for a full retreat. Finally, there was the castle itself, which was the last to fall.*

> In what order did things happen?
>
> A – Castle fell, then retreat, then the walls fell
>
> B – Retreat, castle fell, walls fell
>
> C – Walls fell, retreat, castle fell
>
> D – Walls and castle fell followed by retreat

The answer is C. The events took place in a clear order. First the walls, then the retreat, then the castle fell.

**Rewording of Facts Questions**

These types of questions will ask about facts in the text, but the answers will not have the exact same wording as the passage does. Instead, they will mean the same thing but the wording will be different.

Here is an example of a reworded fact type of question:

> *Apple sales at the local market have been booming. 300 Granny Smith apples, 200 Fuji apples, and 150 Pink Lady apples have been sold in the last week alone. Those numbers are huge compared to what they were before the latest health food craze hit this part of the state. It is very good for apple farmers as well*
>
> QUESTION
>
>     A – More Fuji apples were sold than anything else
>
>     B – More Pink Lady apples were sold than Fuji.
>
>     C – Granny Smith apples were the top seller last week.
>
>     D – People hate Granny Smith apples.

The answer is C. It is clear that they sold the most. This is a simple comparison problem, even without doing any math at all you can see that Granny Smith apples were the bestselling type of apple last week, which is another way of stating what is being said in the prompt.

**Stated Facts Questions**

This type of question primarily relies on facts which are stated in the passage. You should avoid using any outside information for these questions. In addition, your answer will need to say everything that is in the passage with regard to the question itself. Often, you will want to find an answer that uses the exact wording that you found in the passage.

Here is an example of a stated fact type of question:

> *Ten boys went to the church function, along with five girls, six adults, and no children under two years old.*

How many children under two years old went to the church function?

- A - ten
- B - two
- C - three
- D – none

The correct answer here is D. No children under two years old went to the church function.

**Mood and Tone Questions**

Mood and tone questions are about the emotions that are suggested by the content that you have read.

Here is an example of a mood and tone question:

> *It was a beautiful day. The sun was shining and everything was going great. Blue skies and white clouds were everywhere and, best yet, my little cousin and I were at the park together eating cotton candy!*

What emotions does this prompt elicit in the reader?

- A - happiness
- B - sadness
- C - anger
- D - loneliness

It is pretty clear that A, happiness, is the correct answer in this situation. Blue skies, cotton candy, the park? What could be happier than that?

**Purpose Questions**

This type of question concerns itself with the purpose of the passage.

Here is an example of a purpose type of question:

> *Welcome to the manual for your new blender! Here are a few things you need to know to get started using it! Plug in the AC adapter into the nearest wall outlet and then press the power button to turn the blender on.*

What is the purpose of the above prompt?

>    A – to explain the use of the new blender
> 
>    B – to say what the blender is for
> 
>    C – to get someone to buy the blender
> 
>    D – to blend something

A. Obviously. This is an easy one. Typically, though, this type of question is going to be straightforward and relatively easy to answer.

## Technique Questions

Technique questions want you to identify techniques that form the basis of the structure of the passage you have read.

Here is an example of a question of this type:

> *Her eyes were the moon being reflected on a still ocean.*
> 
> What technique was used in the above prompt?
> 
>    A - simile
> 
>    B - metaphor
> 
>    C - onomatopoeia
> 
>    D - exaggeration

The answer is B. That is the best answer. It is not a simile because "like" or "as" are not used.

## Questions about Conclusions

Conclusions questions are about indirect conclusions that you can infer from the text you have read.

Here is an example:

> *The church is running out of money. Unless donations begin to come up and the rise of atheism as a state religion is stemmed, it will be extremely difficult to continue most of the community programs which have evolved over the last fifty years.*

Which of the following is the best conclusion that you can draw based on the text in the prompt above?

    A – less help can be given to the community because of lack of funds

    B – churches are doing great

    C – atheism is stealing money from the church

    D – the church has only been around for fifty years

The answer is A. The entire purpose of the prompt is talking about the church and their lack of funding. It is easy to draw the conclusion spoken about in A, because it is basically stated.

Here is a table outlining the line scores that utilize the paragraph comprehension subtest score for each branch of the military:

| Branch | Line Score |
| --- | --- |
| Army | Clerical, General Technical, Skilled Technical, Operators and Food, Surveillance and Communications |
| Marines | General Technical |
| Navy/Coast Guard | Administrative, Health, Nuclear, General Technical |
| Air Force | Administrative and General |

## 3.2 – Study Information

The general method of study for the paragraph comprehension portion of the test involves studying the individual type of questions that you will encounter in it. Obviously that sounds simpler than it actually is, but this section is, as the word comprehension, a matter of knowing what to prepare for rather than cramming. This section is akin to a "know it or don't know it" type of situation. The best thing to do is know the types of questions, learn the general tips, take practice questions and tests, and read voraciously. Doing those things will give you the best foundation for this subtest.

## 3.2.1 – Main Ideas

The main idea section concerns itself with exactly what you think: the main idea. Main ideas are going to be general statements that sum up what a given passage is about. Information about the paragraph itself is usually specific and provides support for the main idea, which is often outlined in the very first sentence. Sometimes the main idea is referred to as a thesis statement.

The main idea is sometimes stated directly, but not always. If it is stated, it might be referred to as the topic sentence. Usually happening right at the beginning of a paragraph. Usually, the main idea or the topic sentence will not be found in the middle or the end of a passage, but it can be.

Usually, when you are asked to talk about the main idea, the right answer might be worded differently than the way it is stated in the paragraph. If the writer has chosen to not directly state the main idea, you need to figure out what it is by reviewing all of the information in the passage and determining what general point is being made. This is known as "inferring" the main idea.

The first thing you will want to do when you are trying to come up with the main idea for a given prompt is to look at the very first and the very last sentences of the passage. This does *not* mean you should neglect to read the rest of the passage, but those two sentences are generally the most important. Take a look at the following prompt, for example:

> *Local farmers are having trouble watering their crops due to the drought. Since last year, over ten thousand gallons of water have evaporated from the local fields. Combined with the lack of rain, local crops are dying off. Farmers might have reduced crop yields as a result.*

What would be the main idea here? The main idea is right there in the first sentence. "Local farmers are having trouble watering their crops due to the drought." The rest of the paragraph is only supporting evidence for that main point. You should keep in mind, however, that the main idea is not always going to be the one in the first sentence. Sometimes a paragraph is going to build up the main idea before stating it. Take a look at the following prompt for an example of this:

> *Local gardens are beginning to blossom. Bees are buzzing near the flowers and flying around the trees. Kids are beginning to come outside instead of staying inside out of the cold. The sun is warming everything up. Spring is here!*

The main idea in this case is stated in the final sentence, "spring is here". The rest of this paragraph is being used in order to provide some context and supporting evidence for that main idea.

Note: The main idea, again, is not always going to be stated outright. Sometimes it is going to be indirect or implied. One of the answers, however, should obviously be talking about the main idea.

Writers do not always talk about only one specific point, however, so you need to be prepared to identify sub-points in your paragraph. Details are often included which will support the main idea and they will usually be helping you to prove whatever point the main idea is stating.

If you are having trouble coming up with the main idea, you might try attempting to paraphrase the prompt that you are reading. You can do that without even putting a lot of effort into it, simply do it in your head while you read. If you begin doing this with the things that you read now, you will find yourself improving very quickly.

**3.2.2 – Drawing Conclusions**

These types of questions want you to draw conclusions based on what is in the passage. Often, the writer will not directly state the conclusions that you are meant to draw, but they will be indirectly stated. Usually, they are obvious. Take the pieces of information which are in the passage and then put them together to see what sorts of things are implied. The passage usually will not give you an answer to your question directly and the things which are stated directly in the passage are not conclusions. The conclusion is based on the relationships between the information you have been presented.

Take the following prompt, for example:

> *Most burglaries that occur in residential homes are because people neglected to lock their house up properly when they leave. The resulting crimes, thus, are crimes of opportunity.*

What sorts of conclusions can you draw here? Well, there are a few, not all of them are correct, however. Here are some of the possible conclusions you could come up with:

- Some crimes only occur because someone was neglectful of safety.
- Preventing opportunity will prevent crime.
- Most burglaries are caused by residential homeowners.

The last, obviously, is likely a bad conclusion to draw. It is, however, one that you could come up with based on the information contained in the prompt itself.

### 3.2.3 – Stated Facts

These questions are easily the simplest questions on this subtest. All they do is ask you for a fact which was stated in the passage. The wording will be the same. The exact same statement from the answer will be seen in the passage. Do not be tempted to use outside information which is not located inside of the text. The only information that you will be getting here is going to be inside the passage. Again: The information is ONLY about what is contained in the passage and nothing else.

Take the following passage, for example:

> *Fuji apples were originally created by gardeners working in Japan in the 1930s. They are a type of hybrid apple which resulted from a combination of Red Delicious apples and Virginia Ralls Genet apples. They are large, round, and very sweet (especially when compared with some other types of apples).*

Take a moment to look over this and find some of the stated facts that are in this paragraph. Once you have done that, take a crack at the following question:

1. The Fuji apple is an apple that is
    a. large, round, and very sweet
    b. large, round, and yellow
    c. a non-hybrid apple
    d. grown only in Japan

The answer here is A. That is the only fact that is stated directly. It is stated in the very last sentence of the paragraph. What are some other facts that are in this paragraph?

- Fuji apples are a hybrid of Red Delicious and Virginia Ralls Genet
- Fuji apples are sweet when compared to other apples
- Fuji apples originated in Japan
- Fuji apples were originally created in the 1930s

**3.2.4 – Mood and Tone**

The mood and the tone of a given passage are a representation of the emotions that the content is trying to elicit in the reader. When you are faced with these types of questions, you will want to think about the type of language that is being used. Are they happy? Are they sad? You can usually tell immediately. If the skies are said to be dark and it is raining, the mood is likely sad or depressed. If the sun is out and the sky is bright, the mood will likely be happy. Think about how you might feel if you were suddenly dropped into the world of the passage. Whatever emotions you would likely be feeling at that time are the ones you will probably be feeling in the context of the passage itself.

**3.2.5 – Purpose**

Questions about purpose will try and get at what the passage is intended for. What it is aiming to accomplish. Some writings are meant to provide the reader with information. Some are meant to provide instructions on how to do something. Some are persuasive and try to convince the person reading it of something. The purpose would be what the writing wants to do.

When trying to figure out what a passage is purporting to do, you should look at how the various sentences within it connect and relate with one another. If the passage is mostly evidence for the thesis statement, it is likely an argumentative passage. You should readily be able to tell if it is instructional or if it is meant to tell a story. You can practice this by doing it for each paragraph of the things that you read.

The conclusions that you draw about the meaning of a given prompt is what allows you to get to new ideas which are not directly stated in the text. All of the information which is being given to you by the author should be analyzed in order to find inferences that may be present in the text. You can use the example prompt from earlier in order to illustrate this idea:

> *Local farmers are having trouble watering their crops due to the drought. Since last year, over ten thousand gallons of water have evaporated from the local fields. Combined with the lack of rain, local crops are dying off. Farmers might have reduced crop yields as a result.*

One thing you could infer from this text, for instance, is that the additional of rainfall would correct the problem that the farmers are having with their crops. The crops are dying because of the lack of water and the lack of rain. The addition of water/rain would fix this problem. Clearly this is not directly stated by the author, but all of the information required to come to that conclusion is right there in the text.

What are some other things that you might be able to infer from this passage? Here is a brief list of a couple:

- The drought probably began last year.
- The issue is a combination of heat and lack of rain ("evaporated" is the keyword).

### 3.2.6 – Technique

Writing is always organized into some sort of structure. Various techniques are used to do this, and the technique questions on the OAR concern themselves with those techniques. They might ask you how a passage is structured. They might ask about keywords. Often, there are some tells that you can use to try and determine what sort of passage you are reading and these same words can be used to help determine the sequence of events and the purpose of the passage as well.

Words are the key to figuring out the technique being used. Here are some things to keep in mind:

- Narrative technique uses words like "first", "soon", "then", "next", or might provide you with brief time frames of when events are happening.
- Descriptive technique will use spatial descriptions of what is happening and might utilize the senses (sight, sound, taste, touch, smell).
- Look for words that relate things to each other in space like "on", "next to", "beside", "under", etc.
- Comparison is used as a technique with words like "similarly", "like, "same", etc.
- Contrast can also be done, using words like "as opposed to", "on the other hand", "but", etc.
- If information is presented about why things are happening, this can be the technique of cause and effect. Look for things like "since", "because", "resulting in", "so", etc.

In this section, you might also encounter some literary techniques. Some that you have heard of, some that you may not have heard of. Here is a brief rundown of a few of these types of techniques that you can learn:

- **Simile** – A simile is a technique that is used to compare things with the usage of some sort of connecting word (than, so, as, like, etc.).
- **Metaphor** – This is a technique which is meant to compare unrelated things through the use of rhetorical effect.
- **Ellipsis** – The deliberate omission of certain words.
- **Elision** – Omitting letters in speech. This is what leads to the colloquial speech that many people use when texting or chatting online.
- **Hyperbole** – A form of exaggeration.
- **Onomatopoeia** – Using a word to imitate a real sound (such as "boom" for an explosion).

Obviously there are many techniques, but this should give you a good enough basis for what you are likely to find on the OAR.

### 3.2.7 – Sequence of Events

Questions about the sequence of events are exactly how they sound. They are asking about what order the events of the prompt are occurring in. You will want to spend your time looking at the prompt and picking out words that talk about time. These could be words such as "before," "then," "next," "finally," etc. These are the types of words which indicate what events happened and when they happened. This is a relatively simple thing to do and these types of questions are usually not too complicated.

### 3.2.8 – Reworded Facts

Reworded facts are pretty easy to understand. All you need to do is look for facts that have been stated in the prompt to answer the questions. Usually, you will have to pick an answer which means the exact same thing as something which has been stated in the passage itself, though the words will not always be the same.

## 3.3 – Tips

Here are some general tips to help you with the paragraph comprehension section of the OAR:

- Don't bother reading the instructions here. Not only will they be completely obvious based on the questions, but you already know what you will have to do because you have read through this guide. All the instructions will do is tell you something that you already know and waste some of your valuable time.
- There are two ways to go about reading, and you should do both. Quickly skim the passage to get the main idea, then skim the questions. Once that is done, run back through the passage based on the information that is being asked by the questions. Sometimes close reading is not necessary.
- Don't spend a lot of time on individual questions. If you do not know one, go to the next. You can always go back and answer later (on the pen and paper). With less than a minute per question, you simply can't afford to spend your extra time with questions that you don't know the answer to.
- As always with multiple choice tests, narrow down your options as much as possible before choosing something to go with. This will help you if you wind up having to make an educated guess to get the answer.
- Answers have to be based on the information in the given passage only. If it isn't there, then don't take it into consideration. This can be particularly hard to do if you know information that has not been provided. Fight the urge to use that information.
- To quickly improve on this section of the OAR, UP YOUR READING. Read as much as you can. Read things which are not easy for you to read. Expand your vocabulary if possible. Read newspapers, magazines, and books. When you read, make sure you have both a direct and an indirect understanding of the text. In addition, practice your recall when you can by writing down a list of things you remember from the text every time you finish your reading.
- Be confident in the things that you are reading. Most people begin to falter on this section of the OAR because they constantly second-guess the answers that they have come up with or they believe that they are unable to come up with the correct answers on their own. Chances are, you *are* capable of doing coming up with the answers on your own. Chances are, in fact, the first answer you believe is correct *is* the correct answer.

- Combine your study of this subtest information with the information contained in the word knowledge section. Both of these subtests complement each other.
- If you spot the word "never" in one of the answers (or any word like it; "always", "forever", etc.), don't pick that answer. It is very unlikely any answer giving an absolute is going to be the correct one.

## 3.4 – Practice Questions

Prompt 1:
California is in the middle of a long drought. It is said that it would take a full two years for them to fill up the aquifers which have been depleted as a result of this drought. Even so, they are quickly coming up with plans to fight against the lack of water, including building new desalination plants. They have not, however, bothered to spend time cutting back on the amount of water people are allowed to use to water their lawns or, worse yet, golf courses.

1. What is the problem that California is currently undergoing, according to the prompt above?
    a. drought
    b. too much rain
    c. water being stolen
    d. salt water

2. Which of the following figures of speech is being used heavily in the prompt?
    a. onomatopoeia
    b. exaggeration
    c. metaphor
    d. none of the above

3. Why are the desalination plants being built?
    a. to fix the drought
    b. to get more water
    c. to water golf courses
    d. to help people move to higher ground

4. Which of the following is the best description of the drought?
    a. golf courses are drying out
    b. salination plants exist
    c. the aquifer will take two years to fill
    d. it is raining entirely too much

Prompt 2:
   The United States of America has outlined customs and rules about how the flag of the country can be shown and displayed in a respectful and proper way. For one thing, the flag may only be shown during daylight hours (sunrise to sunset). It can be shown at night only if it can be lit up so it is seen clearly even in the darkness. Everywhere that voting is taking place needs to have flags clearly visible. The flag should never touch the floor or the ground. Flags must not be burned or damaged in any way. Flags should also never be utilized for any sort of marketing.

5. John has his flag out at night under a light, it is located on the roof of his car dealership next to a large sign advertising his prices. What did John do wrong?
    a. flag out at night
    b. the flag being used for marketing
    c. flag not visible
    d. flag touching the ground

6. When can the flag be shown at night?
    a. when it is lit
    b. it can't
    c. when it is on the ground
    d. when it is used in images

7. Which situation is allowed?
    a. flag displayed at night
    b. flag displayed during the day
    c. flag on the ground
    d. flag in advertising

8. Which of the following statements is accurate?
    a. Nobody has ever disrespected the flag.
    b. Rules and customs are made to be broken.
    c. The United States places importance on the flag.
    d. The United States does not place importance on the flag.

Prompt 3:

The unspoken truth of the situation was that there really *was* something going on in the house. Even with the trees brushing on the windows and the fact that there was a graveyard behind the house, Janet had never really believed that it was haunted. It was, however, becoming very hard to argue with the fact that there was something odd going on, given the fact that she was currently looking at a mirror floating five feet above the ground.

9. What is the mood and tone of this passage?
    a. matter of fact
    b. happy
    c. sad
    d. depressed

10. What made Janet begin to believe that the house might be haunted?
    a. the ghost
    b. graveyard out back
    c. trees brushing the windows
    d. floating mirror

Prompt 4:

Professional golf players are usually able to hit the ball a bit faster in modern times than they ever could before. There are a couple of reasons for this. For one thing, they are fitter and better conditioned. They have higher strength levels. Beyond that, there is also the fact that modern golfing equipment utilizes different materials?

11. What is one possible reason pro golf players today can hit farther?
    a. they weight train
    b. they use steroids
    c. they are made of iron
    d. they are not old

12. What is one inference you can draw from this?
    a. golf players used to be more conditioned
    b. materials are worse now than before
    c. golf players used to be less conditioned
    d. gravity is different, allowing for faster balls

Prompt 5:
    I took a seat at the end of the hearthstone opposite that towards which my landlord advanced, and filled up an interval of silence by attempting to caress the canine mother, who had left her nursery, and was sneaking wolfishly to the back of my legs, her lip curled up, and her white teeth watering for a snatch.  My caress provoked a long, guttural gnarl.

*Wuthering Heights* by Emily Bronte

13. What response did the dog have to being touched?
    a. curling up
    b. biting her lip
    c. a snarl
    d. sneaking around

14. Why is the narrator caressing the dog?
    a. to get a snack
    b. to fill the silence
    c. so the dog would care for him
    d. because it came in the room

Prompt 6:
    "Her eyes were the moon reflected on a vast ocean of unimagined depth." This is an example of:

15.
    a. onomatopoeia
    b. exaggeration
    c. simile
    d. metaphor

**3.4.1 – Practice Questions Answer Key**

1. A.
2. D.
3. B.
4. C.
5. B.
6. A.
7. B.
8. C.
9. A.
10. D.
11. A.
12. C.
13. C.
14. B.
15. D.

### 3.5 – Review and Takeaways

The paragraph comprehension subtest is one of the most important tests on the OAR. It is one of the ones that figures into your main score on the test. You need to be able to understand the things that the passage is actually saying to you and, beyond even that, you need to be able to pick out and interpret specific facts and techniques which have been utilized in the prompt. This means you will have to be able to draw conclusions from the prompt, pick out main ideas and thesis statements, and analyze the techniques, purpose, and information which is contained within it.

### 3.5.1 – Review

- **Main Ideas –** This section explains how to find the main idea in a prompt and what the prompt is supposed to be about. Thesis statements.
- **Drawing Conclusions –** This section is on how to draw conclusions based on the prompt.
- **Stated Facts –** Questions and tactics for determining facts stated inside of the prompt.
- **Mood and Tone –** How the prompt seems to be written. How it makes you feel.
- **Purpose –** Why the prompt was written.
- **Technique** – Various writing techniques. Styles.
- **Sequence of Events –** The order that the things happen inside of the prompt.
- **Reworded Facts –** Reworded facts are stated inside the prompt itself, but these will typically word them differently. The purpose is the same, but the way things are stated it a little bit different.

### 3.5.2 – Takeaways

This section is not particularly difficult. The more you read and the more you think about what you are reading, the better you will do on this. With only 13 minutes to answer the 15 questions, you will need to be on your toes. One thing you will want to keep in mind, however, is that you need to read through the prompts as quickly as possible and then read the questions. Once that has been done, go back through the prompt and pick out any additional information that is necessary to answer them.

# 4. Mechanical Comprehension

## 4.1 – Introduction

The mechanical comprehension subtest is meant to help determine how well you understand the basics about physics and forces. This section includes things such as work, pressure, hydraulics, and mechanical advantage. Sometimes, the questions you are asked will include an image that you will need to use to answer.

## 4.2 – Study Information

The mechanical comprehension subtest on the OAR is an overview of basic physics, how machines work, and how you can use mechanics to your own advantage. This section is not too complicated and does not go too in-depth into the physics, but it is a section which is important to understand for a number of subspecialties. It is not one of the core tests which goes into calculating your AFQT score.

This section of the OAR consists of 25 questions that need to be answered within 19 minutes.

### 4.2.1 – Materials

Materials are all of the things which are used for building, constructing things, and work. Some of these are better for specific uses than others. Wood is good for building small to medium sized structures and for quick projects. Metal is good for precision projects, things that need to have rigorous standards, and for larger structures. Small containers which are meant to hold things might be made of cardboard, paper, or something similar.

Here are some examples of common materials:

- Steel
- Wood
- Iron
- Glass

- Cardboard
- Paper
- Wool
- Cotton

**Properties**

Different materials have different properties and characteristics. These are important to understand if you want to select the right materials for the right job.

Here are some of the most important material properties:

- **Weight** – The force that is on an object due to gravity. How much force is going to be required to move the object.
- **Density** – Density is a measure of mass per unit of volume. Basically, how much "stuff" is inside something.
- **Strength** – How well the object can maintain the shape that it has when it is being subjected to pressures and forces from the outside.
- **Contraction** – How much the object will shrink when subjected to certain temperatures.
- **Expansion** – How much the object will enlarge when subjected to certain temperatures.
- **Absorption** – A measure of how well a material can pick up and hold liquid that contacts it.
- **Center of gravity** – This is the point of the object where it can be balanced (equal force on all sides).

## 4.2.2 – Structural Support

Structural support is a concept which combines many of the material properties that were discussed in the previous section. It is, generally, a way to take a specific amount of materials and use it in such a way that it is able to support a given amount of weight. Consider buildings, tables, and other common creations. All of these have to hold up a specific amount of weight, but the amount that they can hold up depends on their specific properties.

### 4.2.3 – Fluid Dynamics

Solids and liquids behave in very different ways. This section will explain what differences exist. *Viscosity* is a term which is utilized to describe how easily a fluid is able to flow. This is a term which is particularly important when it comes to engines. Another term which is important to understand is *compressibility*. This is one of the most important concepts in fluid dynamics. Solids can be compressed with relative ease. Liquids, however, cannot be. The pressure of a liquid will spread out amongst the entirety of the liquid and become equal at all points.

The summary of the main points in the study of hydraulics, thus, would be that liquids are very difficult to compress and that pressure is equal throughout a liquid. Pressure, of course, is defined as the force per unit area. Thus, since the pressure is equal everywhere, if you have a small opening at one end of a container, the pressure will be equal to a large opening at the other. So you can use a small force to push on the smaller end and have a large effect on the larger opening.

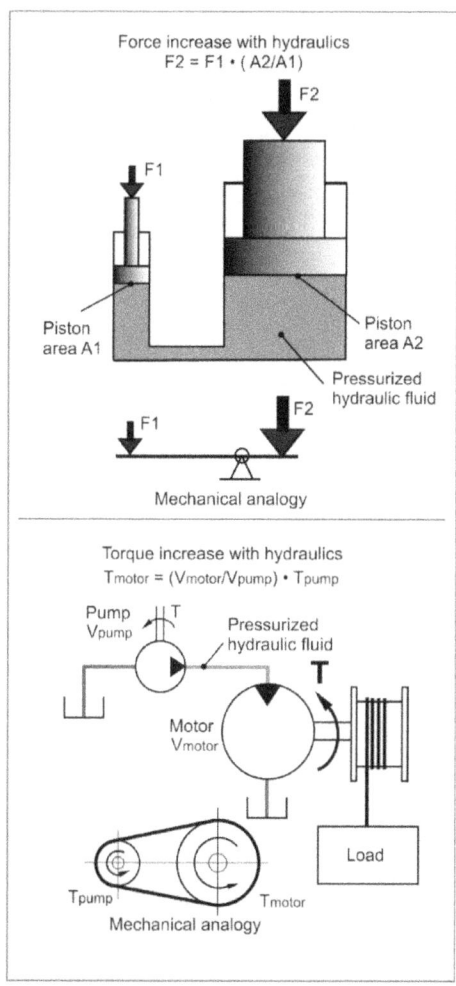

*Common Hydraulic System*

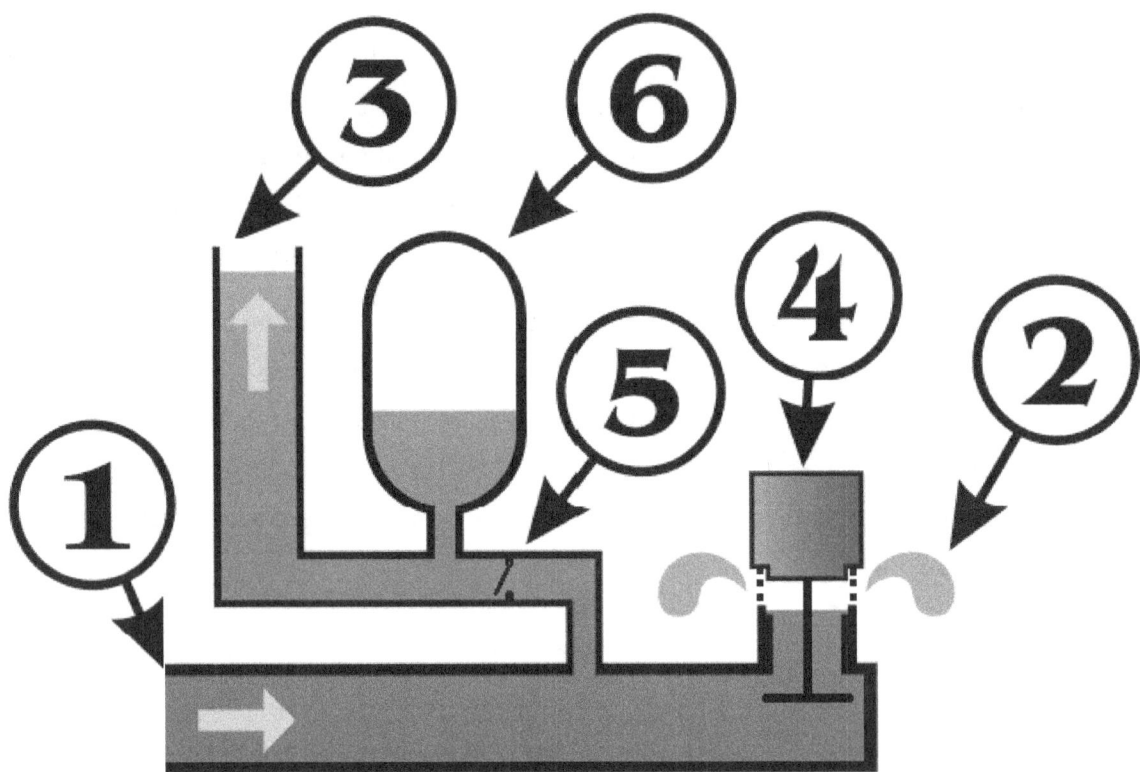

### 4.2.4 – Mechanical Motion

Mechanical motion is a fancy term for just motion. This is the study of how objects move. There are a few terms you will have to understand before getting started with this, some of which have already been covered in this guide.

Here is a brief refresher:

- **Speed** – the total distance traveled divided by the total time required to travel
- **Velocity** – the total displacement divided by the time in which the displacement has taken place.
- **Acceleration** – This is the change in speed divided by the time it takes for the change in speed to occur.

You may be having trouble understanding the difference here, so some clarification may be required. Consider the following scenario:

A car drives around a circular track that has a length of 2 miles. The car drives around the track 3 times in 3 minutes. How fast is the car going?

Well, a total of 6 miles was traveled. 6 miles in 3 minutes is 2 miles per minute. 2 x 60 = 120 or, 120 miles per hour. But the velocity is zero. Why is the velocity zero? Because the car ended exactly where it began. There was no displacement because the track is a circle. This is the primary difference and is a source of confusion. Displacement would be the distance between the ending point and the point that the vehicle started.

Next, you will come to the concept of friction. Two types of friction exist: static and kinetic. Static friction is the type of friction which keeps things from moving. If you are trying to push a heavy crate across the floor and it will not move because of the weight that it carries, you are being prevented from moving due to static friction. Kinetic friction, on the other hand, is the type of friction that slows objects which are already moving. This is why your car will eventually stop moving if you take your foot off the gas.

Engines have a lot of moving parts which have to interact both with other moving parts and with parts of the engine that do not move. The moving parts, during the course of their motion, product kinetic friction. Since the friction is inside the engine, it is called internal friction, which decreases the speed and efficiency of the engine. Oil is used to lubricate engine parts and to help overcome this type of friction.

**Centrifugal Force**

Most people are familiar with what a centrifuge is. If you aren't, then know that it is a machine which has a design that allows it to spin quickly to separate liquids and solids from each other that have been in solution. The reason this works is relatively simple: the machine is spinning but the liquids inside are trying to continue going in a straight line and, thus, are able to separate based on their relative weights.

*Centrifuge*

Retrieved from:
http://upload.wikimedia.org/wikipedia/commons/f/fe/Centrifuge_with_samples_rotating_slowly.jpg

The easiest way to think about this is when you are in a car. If you were to take a fast right turn in a vehicle, what would happen? Your body would feel like it was being pulled to the left. In truth, the car is pulling to the right and your body is just trying to maintain the direction that it was already going (in a straight line).

### 4.2.5 – Simple Machines

Simple machines are utilized in a variety of ways almost universally every single day. These machines are, in truth, something that most people would not even consider machines. To understand how these work, you need to understand the concept of mechanical advantage.

*Mechanical advantage* is a measure of how much a job is being made easier by the assistance of a simple machine.

Here is the formula for calculating mechanical advantage:

R = the distance from the applied force to the pivot point

X = the distance from the pivot point to the magnified force

mechanical advantage = R/X

The first kind of simple machine that you need to understand is the lever. A lever is also referred to as a lever arm. This is going to be a rigid (non-flexible) object which is pivoting around a point. The idea being that force which is applied on one end of the lever will be magnified at the other end.

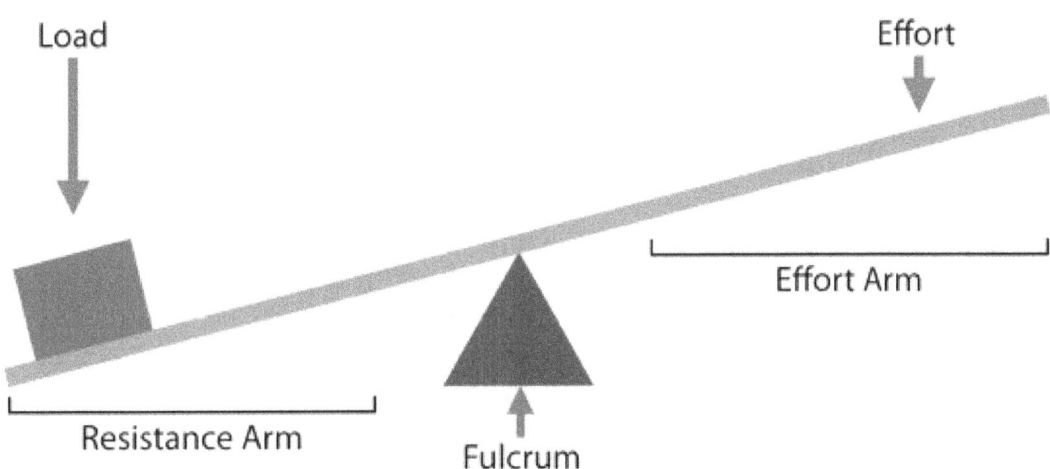

In the image above, when you apply force to the effort arm, the lever will bend about the fulcrum and apply a force to the resistance arm which will be magnified by an amount that can be determined by using the formula for mechanical advantage.

The next type of simple machine that you need to understand is an inclined plane. This is simply a plan which can be used to help you move something from one height to a different height. Usually, these are used to help move heavy boxes or objects from lower points to higher points. Think about this as it is in the real world: a ramp. Pushing a box up a ramp to a height of five feet is a lot easier than picking the box up and lifting it five feet.

# THE INCLINED PLANE

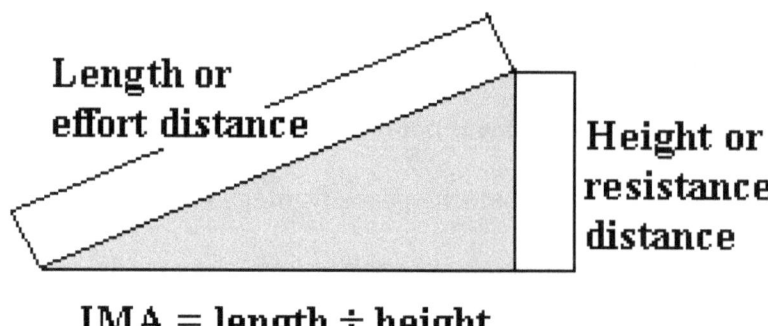

The next type of simple machine is a screw. These are typically used to hold things together, often two pieces of wood or metal. The screw has threads which will hold fast to the material and prevent it from being pulled back out easily.

*Screws*

When looking at the screw in the image above, think about what is happening when it is going into a material. The threads are removing small bits of material, but only enough to fit itself inside. Thus, it sits snugly inside the material.

The next kind of simple machine is a pulley. This is a little bit more complex than the other simple machines that have already been covered. This type of machine has many uses, one of which is helping to lift objects from the ground when used along with a piece of rope.

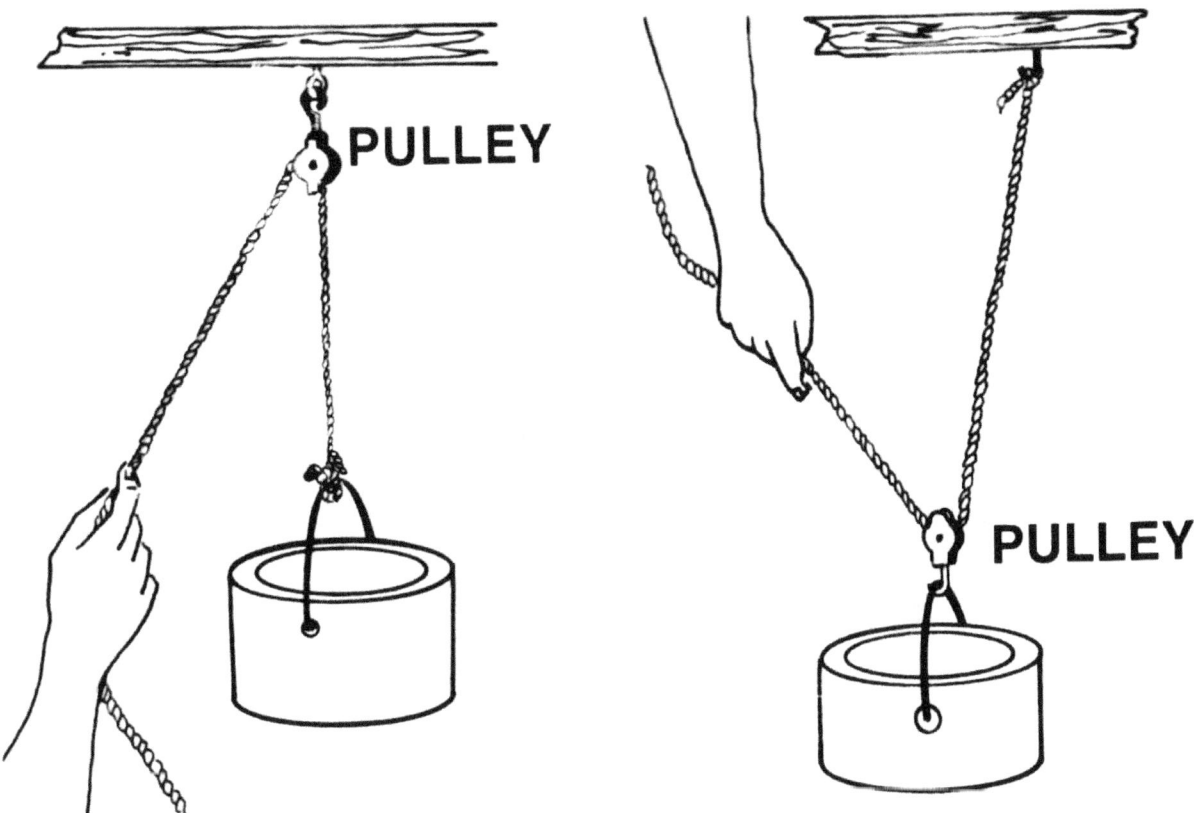

Pulleys are typically used to pull something from one point to a point at a different height easily. Someone might be using a pulley on the ceiling to move a large box from the floor up to a high shelf, for instance. The applied force can be equal to exerted force in some situations. Depending on the exact way that the pulley is being used, the force that you are applying to the pulley can be greatly increased.

The next type of simple machine is a wedge, which is typically utilized to split objects and separate them from each other. A crowbar might be an example of this (and an example of a lever). Another might be a hatchet or an ax. A nail is an example as well.

*Wedge*

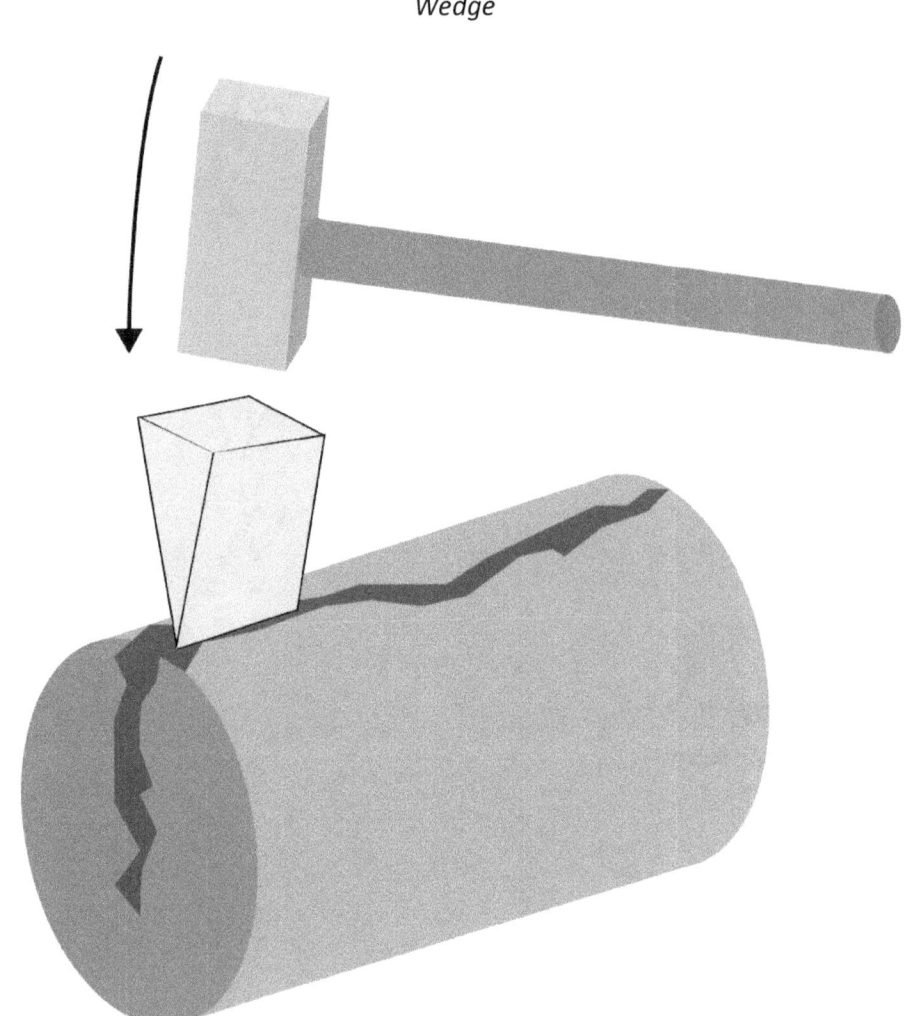

Where the wedge is very thin, it can be inserted and force can be applied to get it to go inside of the object which is to be separated. Once that happens, the width of the wedge increases so that the farther it goes into the object, the more it pushes the object apart. In the image above, you can see how this would work.

The next type of simple machine is the wheel and axle. When force is applied to the axle through the turning of the wheel, the axle will transfer the force. The most common example of this is the faucet used to get water outside of your home (or the steering wheel on your car).

*Wheel and Axle*

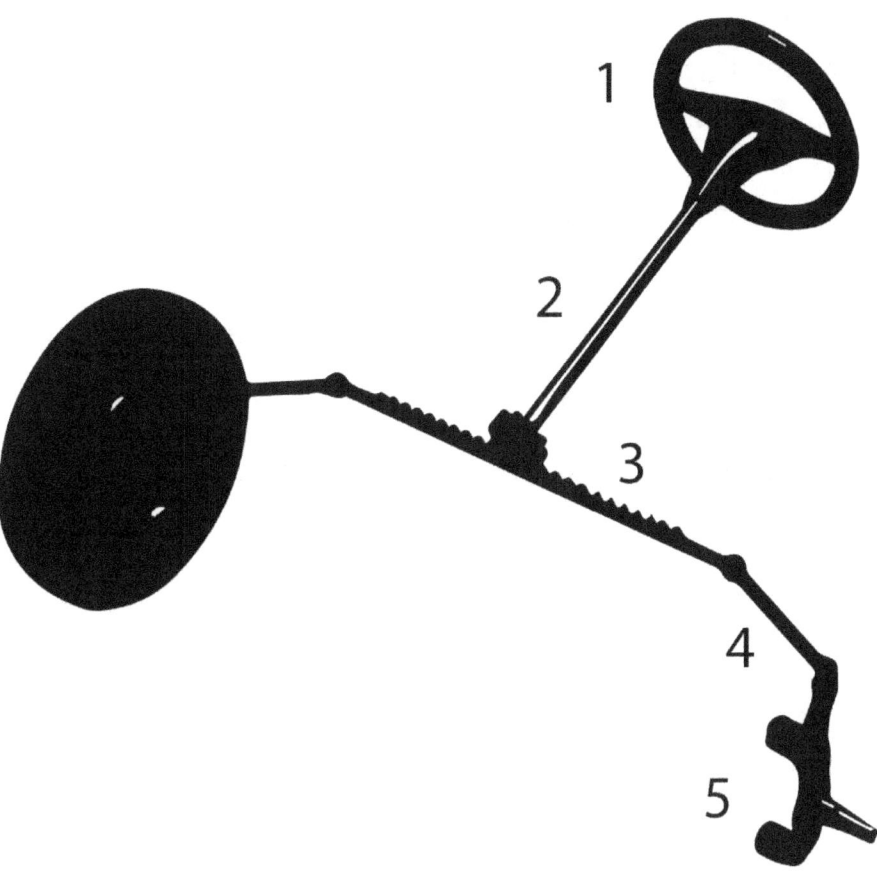

When you turn the steering wheel, the axle that is attached to it will turn the gear on the other end, which will, in turn, move the wheels in the directions you want them to go. This is the basis for the steering in vehicles, among many other things.

### 4.2.6 – Compound Machines

Compound machines are machines which have moving parts and more than one component, usually. These are usually utilized for the same general reasons as simple machines would be. They are meant to allow a mechanical advantage for completing a specific task.

A cam is an example of a compound machine. The cam is going be turned by a piston, thus converting the linear motion of the piston into a circular motion. As the rod turns, it turns the ring which is attached to it. This is the method by which many types of devices work, including combustion engines and certain types of pumps.

Another type of compound machine would be a system of gears. One gear will turn and its teeth will then turn a second gear. Small gears will usually have fewer teeth than large gears, and the number of rotations that each gear goes through in the system will change. The mechanical advantage in this situation is defined by how many teeth the gears have. Divide the number of teeth on the large gear by the number of teeth on the small gear and you will have your mechanical advantage. Gear systems are commonly used in vehicles inside of transmissions.

The next type of compound machine is a crank, which is a rod that has a variable radius that has a chain wrapping around the portion of the rod with the larger radius. This is typically used to help lift a weight. The mechanical advantage in this type of machine is the ratio of the large radius of the rod to the small radius of the rod. A colloquial term which is used to describe this type of machine is "winch".

*Crank*

Another type of compound machine is a linkage, which is a device that is able to convert one type of rotating motion (such as that of a crank) to another type of rotating motion (oscillatory, rotational, or reciprocating). This process, it should be noted, can be reversed. It is not permanent. So you can use a linkage to convert motion in order to turn a crank as well.

*Linkages*

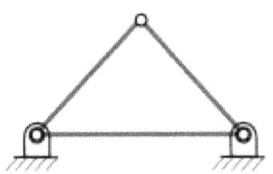 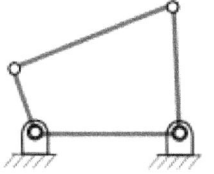 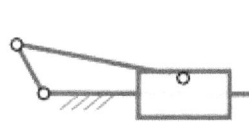 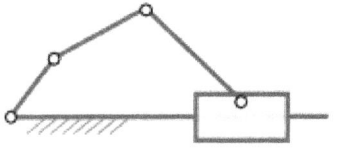

Truss
n=3, f=3, m=0

Four-bar linkage
n=4, f=4, m=1

Crank-slider
n=4, f=4, m=1

Five-bar linkage
n=5, f=5, m=2

## 4.3 – Tips

Here are a few things to keep in mind when you are on the mechanical comprehension subtest of the OAR:

- Don't spend too much time on any single question. Usually, you will either know how to solve it or you won't. Either way you don't have time to waste, so do everything you can as quickly as you can (while still fully understanding what is being asked of you) and go back to the hard ones later if you have the time.
- Narrow down your answers. If you know the answer immediately, mark it down. If you don't, then start ruling out the obviously wrong answers.
- Visualize balance when you are being asked questions with regard to structural support. Often, support will be less stringent if the object you are being asked about is unbalanced.
- When you are being asked questions about fluids, try to figure out whether or not high or low viscosity would be the better choice for use in the system.
- Remember that, when asked about hydraulic systems, the pressure will be equal throughout the system, assuming that the system is of equal height.
- Know the difference between speed, acceleration, and velocity. Velocity and speed are terms which are commonly confused, and you can fully expect to be asked a question that will ensure that you know the difference between the two.
- One of the fastest ways to begin understanding simple and compound machines is to find examples of them and play around to see how they work. Even if you do not understand all of the mechanics, understanding the basic functionality that is coming into play can be enough to answer many questions on the OAR about them.
- Go ahead and cross out answers that you find on the test that you already know are incorrect, that way you won't accidentally spend time reconsidering these questions when you already know they are incorrect.
- Understand the way that mechanical advantage works for different types of machines. Even though the machines themselves are different, the equation is the same. Even so, it is important that you have a good idea in your head of the different forces that you need to look at.
- Understand the different ways that solids and liquids respond to stimuli from the outside. This is the key to understanding materials and their properties. The way they

stand up to the environment is the primary way that you determine which one will be used in what situations.

## 4.4 – Practice Questions

1. Which of the following provides the best definition for what "strength" would be, in terms of materials?
    a. how much weight it can lift
    b. its ability to maintain shape
    c. how heavy it is
    d. how well it can float

2. Which of the following can cause an object to accelerate?
    a. force
    b. speed
    c. mass
    d. time

3. What is the primary distinguishing factor between speed and velocity?
    a. total movement
    b. space
    c. displacement in time
    d. distance

4. In which of the following materials would you find the highest density?
    a. paper
    b. wood
    c. water
    d. gold

5. What type of energy might you have at the top of a roller coaster?
    a. potential energy
    b. frictional energy
    c. momentum
    d. torque

6. What is the center of gravity of an object?
    a. the heaviest point of the object
    b. the point where the object can be balanced
    c. the most unbalanced point
    d. where gravity affects the object the most

7. What is the definition of viscosity?
    a. how viscous a fluid is
    b. how vicious an object is
    c. the ease with which a fluid can flow
    d. how long before a fluid becomes solid

8. Two footballs have been placed 60 centimeters apart. They are identical in every way. Where is the center of gravity relative to the second football?
    a. 30 centimeters away toward football 1
    b. 25 centimeters away toward football 1
    c. 40 centimeters away toward football 1
    d. 60 centimeters away toward football 1

9. In which situation are you using a mechanical advantage to assist yourself?
    a. pushing your car
    b. picking up an apple
    c. removing a nail using a claw hammer
    d. climbing a ladder

10. When would you not need to use a pump?
    a. Move water from the ground to the second floor of a house
    b. Move water downhill
    c. Move water into a pool slightly uphill
    d. Get water out of a large enclosement

11. Which of the following is an example of a simple machine?
    a. a screw
    b. an engine
    c. a radio
    d. a small robot

12. Which of the following is an example of a complex machine?
    a. screw
    b. pulley
    c. incline plane
    d. crank

13. If gear 1 turns clockwise, which way does gear 2 turn (assuming they are connected)?
    a. counterclockwise
    b. clockwise
    c. it doesn't turn
    d. not enough information

14. What kind of force is used to slow down a car?
    a. centripetal
    b. centrifugal
    c. friction
    d. gravity

15. An increase in speed is known as:
    a. deceleration
    b. acceleration
    c. force
    d. velocity

## 4.4.1 – Practice Questions Answer Key

1. B.
2. A.
3. C.
4. D.
5. A.
6. B.
7. C.
8. A.
9. C.
10. B.
11. A.
12. D.
13. A.
14. C.
15. B.

## 4.5 – Review and Takeaways

The mechanical comprehension section of the OAR is primarily used to help the military figure out composite scores so they can place you into a specialty. It is utilized to ensure that you are able to understand how simple and slightly complex machines work, how to utilize forces involved in basic physics, and to employ mechanical advantage when it is of benefit to you to do so. They may show an image and then ask you questions about in on the test in order to make sure you adequately understand specific concepts.

### 4.5.1 – Review

- **Materials** – Different types of materials, the properties of those materials, when they might be used, etc.
- **Structural Support** – Structural support is the primary means by which weight can be held up by a given structure.
- **Fluid Dynamics** – How fluids work. This also covers information about the basics of hydraulics.
- **Mechanical Motion** – How movement works. This includes forces, speed, acceleration, velocity, and information about hydraulics.
    - **Centrifugal Motion** – A type of motion which is used when you need to separate solids from liquids or to separate different substances based on their relative densities.
- **Simple Machines** – Simple, one part machines. Information about screws, planes, wedges, and pulleys, among others.
- **Compound Machines** – Compound machines are machines with moving parts and multiple components.

### 4.5.2 – Takeaways

The entire point of this subtest is to make sure you understand three primary things: how forces interact with objects, how work is done on objects, and how machines work. If you have a broad understanding of these three topics, then you should have no issue with the mechanical comprehension portion of the OAR. Though the machines which are covered here are a bit complicated at times, the basic way that mechanical advantage works does not change. It is important that you understand the concepts here, at least on a narrow and shallow level, to do well on this portion of the OAR. This is especially true when it comes to both hydraulics and mechanical advantage, which are one of the tests favorite types of questions.

# 5. OAR Practice Test #1

## PARAGRAPH COMPREHENSION

Prompt 1:

Young Conrad's birthday was fixed for his espousals.  The company was assembled in the chapel of the Castle, and everything ready for beginning the divine office, when Conrad himself was missing.  Manfred, impatient of the least delay, and who had not observed his son retire, despatched one of his attendants to summon the young Prince.  The servant, who had not stayed long enough to have crossed the court to Conrad's apartment, came running back breathless, in a frantic manner, his eyes staring, and foaming at the month.  He said nothing, but pointed to the court.

*The Castle of Otranto* by Horace Walpole

1. What is the general mood of this passage?
    a. Happy
    b. Depressing
    c. Frantic
    d. Hopeful

2. On which day was Conrad to be married?
    a. The birthday of his wife.
    b. His own birthday.
    c. His father's birthday.
    d. The day after his birthday/

Prompt 2:

In the past, many cars were a manual transmission. Today, however, cars have shifted over to automatic transmission (for the most part). Shifting gears in a manual, however, is an important skill to learn if you plan to hit the road. Simply depress the clutch and then shift with the shifting lever to get the right gear. Then release the clutch and apply pressure to the gas at the same time.

3. Why have cars shifted from
    a. because manuals no longer work
    b. manuals are too complex
    c. to lower costs
    d. not enough information
4. What is the second step in shifting gears in a manual transmission?
    a. press the gas
    b. press the clutch
    c. move the shifting lever
    d. press the brake

5. What kind of transmission are most modern cars?
    a. automatic
    b. manual
    c. shifting
    d. auto gear

Prompt 3:

These visions faded when I perused, for the first time, those poets whose effusions entranced my soul and lifted it to heaven. I also became a poet and for one year lived in a paradise of my own creation; I imagined that I also might obtain a niche in the temple where the names of Homer and Shakespeare are consecrated. You are well acquainted with my failure and how heavily I bore the disappointment. But just at that time I inherited the fortune of my cousin, and my thoughts were turned into the channel of their earlier bent.

*Frankenstein* by Mary Shelley

6. Why did the narrator stop having "visions"?
    a. he discovered poetry
    b. he died
    c. he went to heaven
    d. his soul was lost

7. Where did the narrator live after becoming a poet?
    a. his house
    b. a paradise of his own creation
    c. a temple
    d. none of the above

Prompt 4:

Jim was going to the store to buy apples when he was sidetracked. Sally had been following him the entire time and finally decided to call out. Jim has broken up with her for a reason, and it was ridiculous to think she was still trying to get his attention.

8. Why might Jim not be happy to see Sally?
    a. he is too busy to talk to her
    b. she hates apples
    c. they broke up
    d. she hates him

Prompt 5:

The House of Representatives shall be composed of Members chosen every second Year by the People of the several States, and the Electors in each State shall have the Qualifications requisite for Electors of the most numerous Branch of the State Legislature.

*The United States Constitution*

9. How often are the members of the House of Representatives elected?
    a. every 4 years
    b. every 3 years
    c. every year
    d. every 2 years

Prompt 6:

When in the Course of human events, it becomes necessary for one people to dissolve the political bands which have connected them with another, and to assume among the powers of the earth, the separate and equal station to which the Laws of Nature and of Nature's God entitle them, a decent respect to the opinions of mankind requires that they should declare the causes which impel them to the separation.

*The Declaration of Independence*

10. What is this prompt introducing?
    a. the reasons for a separation
    b. reasons to stay together
    c. a revolution
    d. human history

11. Which of the following might mean the same as "dissolve political bands"?
    a. make a treaty
    b. get rid of the government
    c. abolish slavery
    d. move away

Prompt 7:

Vampires are known to be wary of men who have, on their person, garlic, crosses, holy water, or bibles. They tend to steer clear of these men, as they see them as dangerous to their continued existence.

12. Which of the following do vampires avoid?
    a. garlic
    b. holy water
    c. crosses
    d. all of the above

Prompt 8:

No Senator or Representative shall, during the Time for which he was elected, be appointed to any civil Office under the Authority of the United States, which shall have been created, or the Emoluments whereof shall have been encreased during such time; and no Person holding any Office under the United States, shall be a Member of either House during his Continuance in Office.

*The United States Constitution*

13. What is this meant to state?
    a. Representatives cannot create job for themselves and give themselves those jobs
    b. Representatives cannot be paid
    c. Representatives cannot be civil servants
    d. Representatives must quit their jobs

Prompt 9:

Today was not a good day. It all started with the rain in the morning. The windows were down on the car, so the seats got all wet. Then the call from Juliet, and the breakup. After that, I lost my job. Today was not a good day at all.

14. What was the last sign that "today was not a good day?
    a. rain
    b. car seat
    c. call from Juliet
    d. lost job

Prompt 10:

When Dr. Van Helsing and Dr. Seward had come back from seeing poor Renfield, we went gravely into what was to be done. First, Dr. Seward told us that when he and Dr. Van Helsing had gone down to the room below they had found Renfield lying on the floor, all in a heap. His face was all bruised and crushed in, and the bones of the neck were broken.

*Dracula* by Bram Stoker

15. What does the narrator mean by "went gravely into what was to be done"?
    a. kill each other
    b. go to a grave
    c. dig a grave
    d. make a plan

Prompt 11:

Every year the Academy Awards, or better known as The Oscars, brings together the best of the best in Hollywood. Each year since the original awards ceremony in 1929 great achievements in all areas of the film industry are recognized. Many married female actors, however, shy away from the honor of winning the *Academy Award of Merit* for either Best Actress or Best Supporting Actress. Ever since 1935, the "Oscar Curse" has proven more often than not to be alive and well.

16. What is the "Oscar Curse" that these famous ladies of Hollywood fear?
    a. They fear that after winning they will meet an untimely end.
    b. That soon after winning this prestigious award, the lady's husband will leave them.
    c. The fear is that their next movie will be a box-office disaster.
    d. They fear that once they win one, they will never again win in the same category.

Prompt 12:

According to CNN.com, Google recently announced that it is developing smart contact lenses that will measure a diabetic's glucose level by testing the person's tears. If victorious, Google will eliminate a very laborious daily routine in every diabetic's life; drawing blood from their body (usually from the side of a finger) to test their glucose levels.

17. In this paragraph, what does the word laborious mean?
    a. Consuming too much time
    b. Needing much unwelcome, often tedious, effort
    c. Needing to be done in a medical laboratory
    d. An excruciatingly painful procedure

Prompt 13:

Ikea stores have a unique section in their parking lots. They have a "family friendly" parking area. This area is located very close to the front entrance to the store. These spots have pink strollers painted on each parking spot.

> 18. What is implied by the term "family friendly"?
> a. It is implying that only those customers who come to shop at the store with young children or pregnant women can park in this area.
> b. That if you have an Ikea Family Membership you are welcomed to park in this area.
> c. Any family, of any age, are welcome to park in this special area.
> d. That if there are only a few spots left in this area of the parking lot, it would be nice to leave it for a vehicle with a family but not it isn't necessary; anyone can park there.

Prompt 14:

Everyone dreams of winning the lottery; one million, 25 million, even 55 million dollars. It is very easy to get caught up in the dreams associated with winning the jackpot. The realists of the world, however, are quick to remind us that we have a better chance of being hit by a car than winning big with the lottery.

> 19. What does the comparison of winning the lottery to being hit by a car imply?
> a. That if you don't have the good luck to win the lottery watch out because you only have bad luck and are likely to be hit by a car.
> b. It implies that it is not lucky to either win the lottery or be hit by a car.
> c. The comparison means that more people will get hit by a car than win big with the lottery.
> d. The implication is that if you are going to buy a lottery ticket, don't walk.

Prompt 15:

The United States Military Academy at West Point (USMA) is better known as The Point. Dating back to 1802, this coeducational federal service academy has trained some of the most revered and honored military leaders in American history. West Point has a Cadet Honor Code that is almost as old as the academy itself; "A Cadet will not lie, cheat, steal, or tolerate those who do."

20. What is the foundation of the Honor Code of West Point?
    a. The foundation of the Honor Code comes from a time when the United States where divided by the conflicts leading up to the American Civil War, but were training soldiers from both sides of the Mason-Dixie Line. This Code was required to prevent men from fighting amongst themselves.
    b. This code came from the *Southern Gentleman's Guide to Behavior* and introduced to men from the northern states during the early years of the academy.
    c. The Honor Code of West Point was adopted from the *British Military's Training Manual* that was created years before West Point even existed.
    d. West Point's Code of Honor dates back to the beginning of the academy when a gentle man's word was considered his bond. To break one's word was the worst possible thing a gentleman could ever do. His word was his honor, and without honor a man was nothing.

## MATHEMATICS KNOWLEDGE

1. A woman's dinner bill comes to $48.30. If she adds a 20% tip, what will she pay in total?
    a. $9.66
    b. $38.64
    c. $68.30
    d. $57.96

2. Evaluate the expression $\frac{x^2-2y}{y}$ when $x = 20$ and $y = \frac{x}{2}$.
    a. 0
    b. 38
    c. 36
    d. 19

3. Adam is painting the outside of a 4-walled shed. The shed is 5 feet wide, 4 feet deep, and 7 feet high. How much paint will Adam need?
    a. 126 ft$^2$
    b. 140 ft$^3$
    c. 63 ft$^2$
    d. 46 feet

4. Liz is installing a tile backsplash. If each tile is an equilateral triangle with sides that measure 6 centimeters in length, how many tiles does she need to cover an area of 1800 square centimeters?
    a. 36 tiles
    b. 100 tiles
    c. 50 tiles
    d. 300 tiles

5. $2.31 * 10^2 =$
    a. 23.1
    b. 231
    c. 2310
    d. 23100

6. If $f(x) = |x - 28|$, evaluate $f(-12)$.
    a. $-16$
    b. 40
    c. 16
    d. $-40$

7. $10^8 / 10^3 =$
    e. $10^5$
    f. $10^6$
    g. $10^{11}$
    h. $10^{10}$

8. What is 15% of 986?
    i. 146.9
    j. 98.6
    k. 9.86
    l. 147.9

9. A circular swimming pool has a circumference of 49 feet. What is the diameter of the pool?
    a. 15.6 feet
    b. 12.3 feet
    c. 7.8 feet
    d. 17.8 feet

10. 50% of 94 is:
    m. 42
    n. 52
    o. 45
    p. 47

11. If ∡A measures 57°, find ∡G.

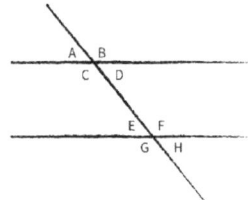

   a. 57°
   b. 147°
   c. 123°
   d. 33°

12. The table below shows the number of hours worked by employees during the week. What is the median number of hours worked per week by the employees?

| Employee | Suzanne | Joe | Mark | Ellen | Jill | Rob | Nicole | Deb |
|---|---|---|---|---|---|---|---|---|
| Hours worked per week | 42 | 38 | 25 | 50 | 45 | 46 | 17 | 41 |

   a. 38
   b. 41
   c. 42
   d. 41.5

13. Multiply the following terms: $(11xy)(2x^2y)$
   a. $13xy + x$
   b. $22x^3y^2$
   c. $44x^3y^3$
   d. $22xy^2 + 2x^2$

14. y = 2x − 5. x = 10. What is y?
   q. 10
   r. 20
   s. 15
   t. 5

15. x=2, y = -3, z = 4. Solve x+y*z
    u.  -4
    v.  10
    w.  -12
    x.  -10

16. Factor the expression $64 - 100x^2$.
    a. $(8 + 10x)(8 - 10x)$
    b. $(8 + 10x)^2$
    c. $(8 - 10x)^2$
    d. $(8 + 10x)(8x + 10)$

17. Which expression would you solve first in the following: (9+9) x 987 + $4^6$
    a. $4^6$
    b. (9+9)
    c. 9 X 987
    d. 987 + 4

18. Solve for y: $10y - 8 - 2y = 4y - 22 + 5y$
    a. $y = -4\frac{2}{3}$
    b. $y = 14$
    c. $y = 30$
    d. $y = -30$

19. Solve for x: $(2x + 6)(3x - 15) = 0$
    a. $x = -5, 3$
    b. $x = -3, 5$
    c. $x = -2, -3$
    d. $x = -6, 15$

20. Round 0.1938562 to the nearest tenth.
    y. 0.0
    z. 0.2
    aa. 0.19
    bb. 0.194

21. Points B and C are on a circle, and a chord is formed by line segment $\overline{BC}$. If the distance from the center of the circle to point B is 10 centimeters, and the distance from the center of the circle to the center of line segment $\overline{BC}$ is 8 centimeters, what is the length of line segment $\overline{BC}$?
    a. 6 centimeters
    b. 4 centimeters
    c. 12 centimeters
    d. 14 centimeters

22. If $f(x) = 3^x - 2$, evaluate $f(5)$.
    a. 27
    b. 243
    c. 241
    d. 13

23. If a spherical water balloon is filled with 113 milliliters of water, what is the approximate radius of the balloon? (Note: The volume, V, of a sphere with radius r is found using the equation $V = \frac{4}{3}\pi r^3$.)
    a. 4.0 centimeters
    b. 3.0 centimeters
    c. 3.6 centimeters
    d. 3.3 centimeters

24. Simplify 13/26 into a decimal.
    a. 0.13
    b. 0.16
    c. 0.5
    d. 0.25

25. Factor the expression 100x^2+25x.
    a. 100x(x+25x)
    b. 25(4x+x)
    c. 25x(4x+1)
    d. 25(4x^2+x)

26. F(x)=6x-3, G(x)=3x+4
    What will be F(3)-G(2) equal to?
    a. 4
    b. 3
    c. 5
    d. 2

27. The mean of the marks obtained by the students in a class is 60 out of 100, and the standard deviation is 0. It means that
    a. Half of the students have scored marks less than 60
    b. Half of the students have scored marks greater than 60
    c. No student has scored 100 marks
    d. All the students have scored 60 marks each

28. $0.00092 \times 10^{-3}$ is equal to which of the following?
    a. $0.000093 \times 10^{-4}$
    b. $0.000092 \times 10^{-2}$
    c. $0.000000092$
    d. $0.92 \times 10^{-8}$

29. The remainder is 3 when we divide one number by another number. What can be these two numbers from the following?
    a. 9, 5
    b. 8, 5
    c. 9, 6
    d. both B & C

30. If A and B are odd integers. Which of the following expressions must give an odd integer?
    a. A×B
    b. A+B
    c. A-B
    d. Both options A & C

# MECHANICAL COMPREHENSION

1. What is the formula that is used to calculate work?
    a. W = F * s
    b. W = v * F
    c. W = P * s
    d. W = P * F

2. If an engine with a power output of around 2 horsepower is 95% efficient, what would the actual power output be, in horsepower?
    a. 190
    b. 95
    c. 1.90
    d. 0.19

3. A class 2 lever has the load placed between the fulcrum/pivot point and the effort being placed on it. Which of these might be an example of this?
    a. wheelbarrow
    b. gun
    c. wrench
    d. screwdriver

4. One of the following materials is a ceramic, which one is it?
    a. dirt
    b. gold
    c. pots
    d. brick

5. Force per unit of distance is a description of what?
    a. velocity
    b. force fields
    c. power
    d. work

6. Which one of the following might be a good example of a simple machine?
    a. ladder
    b. drill
    c. jackhammer
    d. iPod

7. A machine is operating with an input (for work) of 215-foot pounds. The output of the work for this machine is 204.25-foot pounds. What efficiency does this machine have, considering the information above?
    a. 90%
    b. 95%
    c. 100%
    d. 200%

8. If there are 20 lbs. on one side of a fulcrum (with equal lengths on both sides), which of the following combinations of weights would be enough to balance the loads on that fulcrum?
    a. 18 and 1
    b. 18 and 2
    c. 18 and 3
    d. 12 and 18

9. What kind of machine would a cam be considered?
    a. difficult
    b. simple
    c. conductor
    d. compound

10. How would you find an exerted force?
    a. find the force using the formula for work
    b. use the force field formula
    c. multiply applied force by the ratio of the areas to which it is being applied
    d. none of the above

11. What is a linkage?
    a. a way of converting rotating motion of a crank
    b. a type of fence
    c. a way to move chains
    d. a pulley system of complex design

12. Which of the following is a description of mechanical advantage?
    a. input force * output force
    b. output force * input force
    c. output force / input force
    d. input force / output force

13. If someone puts in 50 newtons of force and gets back 250 newtons of force, then what is the mechanical advantage?
    a. 5
    b. 10
    c. 15
    d. 20

14. What is the name of the force between objects that attracts them together?
    a. friction
    b. gravity
    c. force
    d. power

15. What might cause an object to accelerate?
    a. force
    b. gravity
    c. pulling on it
    d. all of the above

16. What amount of force would have to be applied to move a box 25 meters? 55,000 joules worth of work is utilized in the process of moving the box.
    a. 2500 newtons
    b. 4000 newtons
    c. 2200 newtons
    d. 5500 newtons

17. What is heat?
    a. a type of motion
    b. a type of pressure
    c. a type of energy
    d. the result of friction

18. If two liquids that have different densities are mixed together, what will happen?
    a. they will separate
    b. they will combine into one fluid
    c. they will react violently
    d. they will flow out of the container

19. What is the SI unit that is commonly used to measure mass?
    a. liter
    b. kilograms
    c. newtons
    d. all of the above

20. When would a spring likely be utilized?
    a. when making a large volleyball
    b. when creating a football
    c. when making a new baseball bat
    d. when building a pogo stick

21. When people are using a seesaw, the seesaw will work most efficiently if the two people have the same weight. Why?
    a. principle of equilibrium
    b. principle of force
    c. Newton's law
    d. the first law of motion

22. Shock absorption on vehicles is attributed to what?
    a. elasticity of springs
    b. brakes
    c. the engine block
    d. the weight of the vehicle

23. What type of device would you compare a crane to?
    a. car
    b. elevator
    c. pulley
    d. lever

24. If you were going to make something that was solid but would not float, what might you use?
    a. plastic
    b. glass
    c. metal
    d. wood

25. How do brakes slow vehicles down?
    a. force
    b. combustion
    c. acceleration
    d. friction

26. Which of the following is not a correct unit for the amount of work done:
    a. Joule
    b. Horsepower-hour
    c. Calorie
    d. Newton

27. Observe the figure:

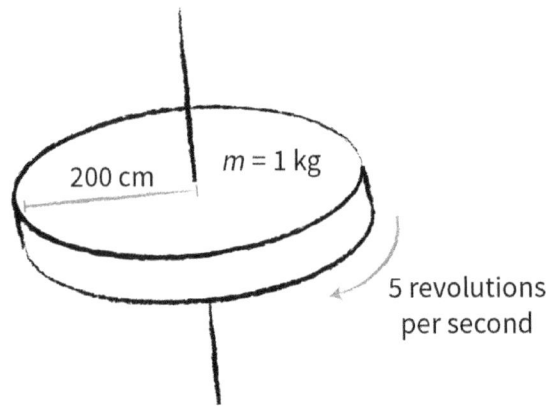

The kinetic energy of the disc is:
a. $80 \pi^2$ J
b. $100 \pi^2$ J
c. $125 \pi^2$ J
d. $144 \pi^2$ J

28. Consider the following figure of a rolling wheel on smooth horizontal surface:

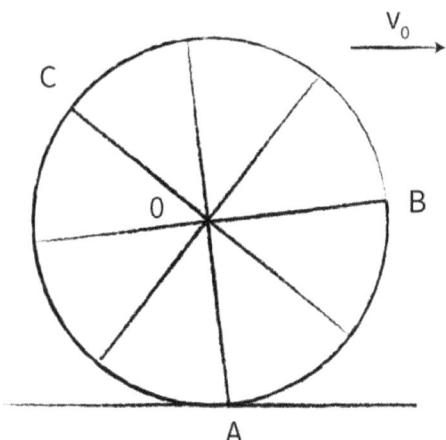

Then,
   i. Speed at the point A is 0
   ii. Speed at point B & C = $v_0$
   iii. Speed at point B > Speed at point O

   a. All the statements are true
   b. Only statement (i) & (ii) are true
   c. Only statement (i) & (iii) are true
   d. Only statement (ii) & (iii) are true

29. In the following figure, consider a block of mass m. What is the ratio of the force required, for a person to lift the block upwards with & without a pulley? (Hint: Assume F=T)
   a. 2
   b. 1/3
   c. 3
   d. ½

30. A block of mass 3kg lies on a horizontal surface with µ = 0.7, select the force closest to what is required just to move the block:
   a. 15N
   b. 21N
   c. 18N
   d. 24N

## 5.1 – OAR Practice Test #1 Answer Key

**PARAGRAPH COMPREHENSION**

1. C.
2. B.
3. D.
4. C.
5. A.
6. A.
7. B.
8. C.
9. D.
10. A.
11. B.
12. D.
13. A.
14. D.
15. D.
16. C.
17. B.
18. A.
19. D.
20. D.

# MATHEMATICS KNOWLEDGE

1. B.
2. B.
3. A.
4. B.
5. B.
6. B.
7. A.
8. D.
9. A.
10. D.
11. C.
12. D.
13. B.
14. C.
15. D.
16. A.
17. B
18. B.
19. B.
20. B.
21. C.
22. C.
23. B.
24. C.
25. C.
26. C.
27. D.
28. B.
29. D.
30. A.

## MECHANICAL COMPREHENSION

1. A.
2. C.
3. A.
4. D.
5. D.
6. A.
7. B.
8. B.
9. D.
10. C.
11. A.
12. C.
13. A.
14. B.
15. D.
16. C.
17. C.
18. A.
19. B.
20. D.
21. A.
22. A.
23. B.
24. C.
25. D.
26. D.
27. B.
28. C.
29. D.
30. B.

# 6. OAR Practice Test #2

## PARAGRAPH COMPREHENSION

Prompt 1:

Davy Crockett is one of America's best-known folk heroes. Known for his political contributions to the State of Tennessee and the U.S. Congress, he also became famous during his own time for "larger than life" exploits that were retold through plays and in almanacs. Even following his death, Davy Crockett became growingly famous for exploits of legendary magnitude.

1. In this paragraph, what is the meaning of the word "almanacs"?
    a. An almanac is a book of information including a calendar, weather based predictions, anniversaries, and important events that is published yearly.
    b. An Almanac is another name for a book of locally developed plays that is published every couple years or so.
    c. An Almanac is a series of comics based on popular folklore that is published every five years.
    d. An almanac is a name given to stories that are handed down from one generation to another orally, not by written word.

Prompt 2:

Rosa Parks was a civil rights activist who refused to give up her seat in the colored section on a city bus for a white person when the white section of the bus was full and was subsequently arrested. *My Story*, which is her autobiography, she is quoted as saying, "People always say that I didn't give up my seat because I was [physically] tired [or] old….No, the only tired I was, was tired of giving in."

2. What implied by this quote?
    a. That she was old and tired of walking home after work each day and finally gave in and paid to take the bus home.
    b. This quote implies that Rosa Parks was not tired physically, or too old to stand on a bus, she was just tired of having to give in to the demands of white people; she was tired of segregation based on race.
    c. This quote means that people thought Rosa Parks was just too lazy to give up her seat on the bus.
    d. Rosa Parks was just stubborn that day on the bus, and her actions had nothing to do with the civil rights movement.

Prompt 3:

One island from the shores of San Francisco Bay is often referred to as "The Rock"; Alcatraz Island. The island has been home to one kind of prison or another since 1861 up until 1963. During its time as a federal prison, it is stated that no prisoner successfully escaped from Alcatraz although there were 14 attempts in that time.

3. Why were there never any successful escapes from the prison on Alcatraz Island?
    a. No one ever successfully escaped the prison because there were too many guards on duty. No man was ever left alone when outside of his cell.
    b. Alcatraz was inescapable because even if they penetrated the high-security around the prison, there was no way off the island since no boats were ever docked at the wharf.
    c. The entire premise of Alcatraz was that the men sent here were not to be rehabilitated back into society. Each and every aspect and component of the prison, the training of the guards, and the security around the rest of the island was created with the idea of keeping them on the island forever.
    d. The majority of men at the time the prison was active did not know how to swim, so those who attempted drowned in the water if they were not caught first.

Prompt 4:

When one wants to train a house-dog to ring a bell instead of barking to let its owner know it wants to go outside, there are only a few simple steps. First, when the dog is at the door, and barks take its paw and knock it against the bell that is hanging from the doorknob and only then open the door and let the dog outside. Repeat this every single time the dog barks to go outside. Eventually, depending on the stubbornness of the animal, the dog will cease barking at all and go to the bell and ring it each time it wants to go outside.

4. What is the type of training called?
    a. This type of training is called Negative Behavior Elimination Training.
    b. This training is referred to as either Classical Conditioning or Pavlovian Conditioning.
    c. This training called Positive Reinforcement Training.
    d. This type of training is called Basic Cognitive Retraining.

Prompt 5:

When we think of "rights" we think in terms of Human Rights. This refers to ideas that apply to everyone, everywhere in the world. These expectations are egalitarian and are part of a declaration called the *Universal Declaration of Human Rights* that adopted by the U.N. General Assembly in 1948 after the end of WWII.

5. In this paragraph, what does the word "egalitarian" mean?
    a. This word means that the rights contained in the *Universal Declaration of Human Rights* are to all be taken literally.
    b. Egalitarian means that ultimately these rights will also be applied to immediately to anyone and everyone who requests to be treated fairly.
    c. This word means that examples of basic human rights are included in the declaration adopted by the U.N.
    d. The word egalitarian means that Human Rights are the same for everyone, regardless of their race, nationality, or any other factors.

Prompt 6:

Each branch of the United States Armed Forces has special mottos that the soldiers live and are expected to die by. These special expressions are points of extreme pride for each member of the military.

6. What is the motto of the United States National Guard?
    a. "This We'll Defend"
    b. "Always Ready, Always There"
    c. "That Others May Live"
    d. "Not Self, but Country"

Prompt 7:

Examples of colloquialisms include Facebook, y'all, gotta, and shoulda.

7. What is the definition of a colloquialism?
    a. Words that are only used by Americans who live in the south.
    b. Words that only uneducated people say.
    c. Words that are used in an informal conversation, not a more formal discussion.
    d. Words that have recently been added to the dictionary as acceptable words to use in the American English Language.

Prompt 8:

Lieutenant Hiroo Onoda was a Japanese soldier who was sent to a small island in 1944 as an emissary. He refused to believe that Japan surrendered in WWII until his commanding officer finally traveled back to the island in 1974 and finally convinced him that the defeat was real. He then returned to Japan and received a hero's welcome.

8. In this sentence what is the definition of emissary?
    a. Emissary refers to Hiroo Onoda being an ambassador for the Japanese army.
    b. In this sentence, emissary means a secret agent or spy.
    c. The word emissary means messenger in this sentence.
    d. Emissary, in the context of this sentence, means a delegate of the Japanese government meant to establish an embassy on the island.

Prompt 9:

Milton S. Hershey was the founder of North America's largest chocolate manufacturer, now known as, The Hershey Company. It is hard to believe that, with such a large, successful business, that Hershey's first attempts in the confectionary business were such failures. After finishing a confectionary apprenticeship, he opened his own candy shop in Philadelphia; 6 years later it went out of business. He then returned home after failing to manufacture candies in New York City and in 1903 construction of a chocolate plant began in his hometown which was later renamed Hershey, Pennsylvania.

9. What is the main message of this passage?
    a. As an entrepreneur, if your first idea fails, do not give up, but move on to your next plan for success.
    b. One can only be successful in starting a flourishing business with the support of your hometown.
    c. It is more successful to manufacture chocolate than candy.
    d. If you start a worldwide profitable business in your hometown, they will rename the town in your honor.

Prompt 10: *"Beware the leader who bands the drums of war in order to whip the citizenry into a patriotic fervor, for patriotism is indeed a double-edged sword."* This quote of Caesar's is completely anachronistic.

10. What does anachronistic mean in this context?
    a. This word means stolen in this sentence. This is a quote from another ruler from the time of Caesar, but not Caesar himself.
    b. Anachronistic means a quote that is pieced together from parts of speeches made by an individual. It is, therefore, a quote without any real meaning.
    c. In this sentence, the word anachronistic means that this is a true and accurate quote; not a paraphrase.
    d. The word anachronistic is defined as a quote that is not historically accurate in its context. At the time of Caesar; there were no drums of war, for example.

Prompt 11:

*"A stitch in time saves nine."* This is a proverbial expression that has used for hundreds of years.

11. What is this phrase referring to?
    a. This expression means that there is a "rip" of some sort in time and space and that only by repairing this rip will we save the world.
    b. When this phrase is used, the person means that by repairing a piece of clothing, you will save $9.00 on replacing the garment.
    c. This phrase refers to a broken relationship. If it is not repaired in time, it will take years (maybe even 9 years) to mend.
    d. The literal meaning of this expression means that if you stitch something up in time, you will save 9 stitches later. In other words, if you don't procrastinate, and repair something as soon as it is required, you won't have a bigger or worse job to fix at a later time.

Prompt 12:

In the Shakespearean play, *Julius Caesar*, a soothsayer calls out to Caesar with the following quote; *"Beware the Ides of March!"*

12. What did this declaration of the soothsayer mean?
    a. The soothsayer was warning the ruler of his impending betrayal and death at the hands of some of his most trusted men.
    b. This phrase was actually warning the crowd, not Caesar that on ever Ides of March the ruler must choose one human sacrifice to offer up to the Roman gods to guarantee prosperity for the coming year.
    c. The Ides of March was a day of celebration in the Roman Empire to commemorate the deaths of the Christians in the Coliseum. The soothsayer was merely thanking Caesar for the day of celebration. The word "Beware" has been shown to be translated incorrectly into English.
    d. The soothsayer meant to warn Caesar not to upset or anger the god for whom the month of March was named; Mars, the god of war. To upset the god Mars, was to ensure plague, famine, or other ruin.

Prompt 13:

Tornados occur when air begins to rotate and comes into contact with both the earth and a cloud at the same time. Although the size and shape of tornados vary widely, one can usually see a funnel stretching from the sky down to land. Most tornados are accompanied with winds as fast as 110 miles per hour and extreme ones can have winds as fast as 300 miles per hour. The path of a tornado is hard to predict, but it is becoming possible to detect them just before or as they form with the continued collection of data through radar and "storm chasers".

13. Storm chasing is a dangerous profession so why do people continue to put their lives in danger this way?
    a. Storm Chasers are an interesting breed of people who seek the thrill and adventure that comes along with this profession, much like extreme sports.
    b. News channels will pay large sums of money for good video of tornados, so, although it is a dangerous profession, the money is worth the risk.
    c. It is very important to discover as much as possible about how tornados work so that ultimately, scientists will detect them earlier and give people more advanced warning to get to safety. More advanced warning is the only way more lives will be saved.
    d. For statistics reasons, it is important to get first-hand data during a tornado. This way they can be compared to other natural disasters such as hurricanes and tsunamis.

Prompt 14:

"Secret Santa Sings Special Song for Sweetheart" is an example of alliteration.

14. What does "alliteration" mean?
    a. Alliteration means that the sentence has more than one meaning.
    b. Alliteration means that people with a stutter would have difficulty saying this sentence.
    c. Alliteration means that most of the words in the sentence begin with the same letter.
    d. In this sentence "alliteration" means that a secret Santa *literally* sang a special song for his sweetheart; it means that this even actually happened.

Prompt 15:

The Schneider Family was not your average family. Three generations lived in one house; Mom and Dad, four of their children, and Mom's parents who were well into their "golden years."

15. The term "golden years" is a nice way of meaning what?
    a. The term "golden years" refers to the best years of someone's life.
    b. This phrase means that the mom's parents were old or elderly people.
    c. "Golden years" is another way of saying, when they were rich.
    d. In this paragraph, the meaning of the term "golden years" means that the grandparents were spending their years taking care of everyone else in the family.

Prompt 16:

Jim had been on the road for 36 hours straight to meet an important client and hopefully finalize a huge new account for his advertising agency. After checking into his hotel, he intended just to drop off his suitcases and go down to the restaurant for a late supper. Once he entered the room, however, the cozy couch looked so friendly and welcoming to the weary traveler. Personification is a literary device that gives human characteristics to a non-human object.

16. What phrase in this paragraph is an example of personification?
    a. An example from this paragraph that is personification is, "the cozy couch looked so friendly and welcoming…."
    b. "Jim had been on the road for 36 hours straight…." is an example of personification in this paragraph.
    c. The phrase, "…and hopefully, finalize a huge new account for his advertising agency." is an example of personification.
    d. An example of personification, in this paragraph, is, "…to just drop off his suitcase and go down to the restaurant…."

17. Of the phrases below, which one is an example of an oxymoron?
    a) Three of the employees were "let go" due to suspicion of stealing money from the cash drawer.
    b) The stormy night was perfect for this woman's current mood.
    c) It was raining "cats and dogs" when the school bell rang.
    d) The community center was collecting "useless treasures" for their upcoming garage sale.

Prompt 17:

Between April 1860 and October 1861 **The Pony Express** delivered mail, news, and other forms of communication from Missouri across the Great Plains, through the Rocky Mountains, through the desert lands of Nevada to California, using only man and horse power. The Pony Express closed in October of 1861; just two days after the transcontinental telegraph reached Salt Lake City, therefore, connecting Omaha, and Nebraska to California. Other telegraph lines connect many other cities along the Pony Express Route.

18. Why did the Pony Express close?
    a. The Civil War stopped them from running their business.
    b. Another company was faster and took over the business.
    c. The Pony Express riders were unable to pass through the Rocky Mountains in the winter months.
    d. With the transcontinental telegraph connecting so many cities along the route, the Pony Express became redundant.

Prompt 18:

Between 1914 and 1935, George Herman "Babe" Ruth Jr. was known as "the Bambino" to baseball fans. Over his 22 seasons, he only played for three teams (Boston Red Sox, New York Yankees, and Boston Braves) and was known most for his hitting skills and RBI's statistics. Due mostly to Babe Ruth's hitting ability baseball changed during the 1920's from a fast-playing game with lower scores to one of higher scores and a slower pace.

19. How did "The Bambino's" hitting skills and RBI's statistics affect the way baseball was played?
    a. He hit so many batters in that the game went faster.
    b. The innings lasted longer with so many batters scoring runs.
    c. They had to stop the game because every time Babe Ruth hit a home run fans mobbed him.
    d. 'The Regulations changed which caused the game to last longer.

Prompt 19:

**Kraft Macaroni and Cheese** goes by many names. In Canada, it is called Kraft Dinner and in the United Kingdom it is known as Cheesy Pasta. No matter what name it is called by, this pasta dish has been a staple of the typical North American diet since its beginning in 1937. James Lewis Kraft, a Canadian living in Chicago struck gold by introducing this product during WWII, when more and more women were working outside of the home, milk and other dairy foods were rationed and hearty "meatless" meals were relied upon.

20. Why has this product continued to be a staple in our diet over 75 years after it was introduced to Americans?
    a. Most Americans love pasta and cheese.
    b. It is still the cheapest pasta on the market.
    c. The same factors that made its introduction so popular still exist today.
    d. It is still popular today because of brilliant marketing strategies.

# MATH KNOWLEDGE

1. $\frac{4}{5} \div \ldots\ldots = 2$
   
   Which of the following will fill the blank?
   a. $\frac{2}{5}$
   b. $\frac{5}{2}$
   c. $\frac{1}{5}$
   d. Both A & C

2. Given is a set {2, 4, 6, 8……..50}
   How many numbers in the given set are completely divisible by 3?
   a. 6
   b. 8
   c. 7
   d. 9

3. What will be the area of the shaded region in the given figure?

   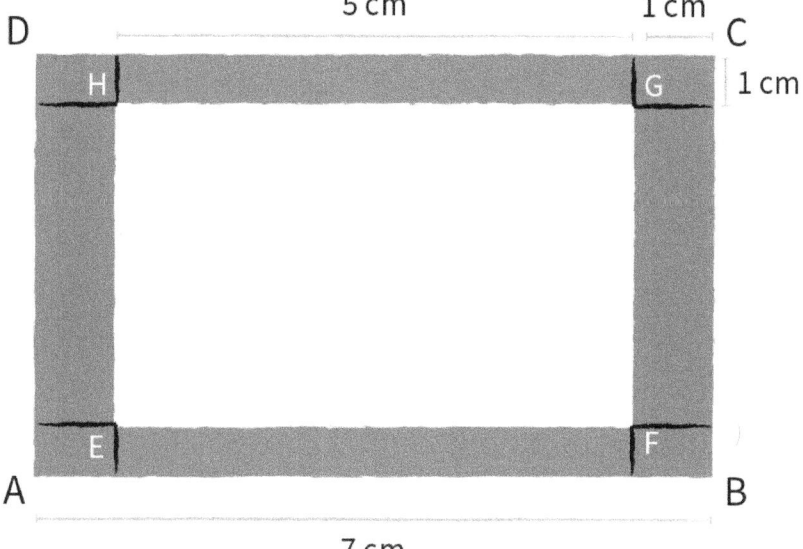

   a. 24 cm²
   b. 26 cm²
   c. 23 cm²
   d. 28 cm²

4. If 2x-y+6 = 2 then what will be the value of "6x"?
    a. 3y+12
    b. y-12
    c. y+12
    d. 3y-12

5. A point is located in coordinate system at (1, 2). What will be the location of this point if it is shifted 5 units downwards and 3 units in the right direction?
    a. (6, -1)
    b. (-4, 5)
    c. Remains same
    d. (4, -3)

6. $\dfrac{y+2}{3y^2+2y} + \dfrac{2y-1}{6y^3+4y^2} =$ .............
    a. $\dfrac{2y^2+6y-1}{6y^3+4y^2}$
    b. $\dfrac{2y^2+8y-1}{6y^3+4y^2}$
    c. $\dfrac{2y^2+6y-1}{3y^2+2y}$
    d. $\dfrac{2y^2+8y-1}{3y^2+2y}$

7. If each side of the square has been increased by 1 cm and the area has now become 36cm². What will be the length of one side of the square before?
    a. 4 cm
    b. 5 cm
    c. 6 cm
    d. 7 cm

8. $(9)^{-3} =$ ........
    a. $\dfrac{1}{9}$
    b. $-\dfrac{1}{(9)^3}$
    c. $\dfrac{1}{(9)^{-3}}$
    d. $\dfrac{1}{(9)^3}$

9. What is the degree of polynomial $5x^2y - 5x^2y^2 + 5x^3y^2$?
    a. 12
    b. 4
    c. 8
    d. 5

10. Which one of the following numbers is not divisible by 3?
    a. 2352
    b. 3243
    c. 6143
    d. 5232

11. (3-x)(3+x) = ........
    a. $9-x^2$
    b. $x^2-9$
    c. $9+x^2$
    d. $x^2-6x+9$

12. Which of these are parallel lines?
    a. x=2, y=3
    b. y=-1, x=4
    c. x=1, x=6
    d. x=9, y=100

13. Which of these are complementary angles?
    a. 63° and 29°
    b. 56° and 38°
    c. 33° and 57°
    d. 46° and 49°

14. The triangle whose one angle is greater than 90 degrees is called ............
    a. Equilateral Triangle
    b. Isosceles Triangle
    c. Scalene Triangle
    d. Obtuse Triangle

15. a×(b+c) = .......
    a. ab+bc
    b. cb+ac
    c. ab+ac
    d. abc

16. Which of the following options is true for Equilateral Triangle?
    a. Three Congruent Angles
    b. Three Congruent Sides
    c. Two Congruent Angles
    d. Two Congruent Sides

17. If $\frac{20-x}{4} = 3y$. What will be x in terms on y?
    a. 20-12y
    b. 20+12y
    c. 12-20y
    d. 12+20y

18. If 38 is divided by m then the remainder is 2 and the quotient is 12. What will be the value of "m" then?
    a. 2
    b. 3
    c. 5
    d. 4

19. If y = 7x, x = 3z. What will be the value of y if z = 2?
    a. 40
    b. 44
    c. 48
    d. 42

20. $4\frac{4}{6} + 2\frac{1}{3} - 1\frac{3}{4} \times 3\frac{2}{5} = $ .............
    a. $\frac{22}{20}$
    b. $\frac{24}{20}$
    c. $\frac{21}{20}$
    d. $\frac{25}{20}$

21. Which one of the following options shows the correct answer of y with respect to its equation?
    a. If 2(y-1)+6=0, then y= 2
    b. If 3(y-3)=3, then y=4
    c. If 2(y+2)=6, then y=-1
    d. If 6y-18 = 6, then y=5

22. A = $x^2$+3x-4, B = $2x^2$-2x+3. What will be the value of "B-A"?
    a. $x^2$-5x+7
    b. $3x^2$-x-1
    c. $x^2$-3x+7
    d. $x^2$-5x-7

23. Pythagorean Theorem is applicable to which one of the following triangles?
    a. Equilateral Triangle
    b. Acute Triangle
    c. Obtuse Triangle
    d. Right-Angled Triangle

24. x=3 is the solution of which one of the following equations?
    a. 6(x+3)-12 = 0
    b. 8(x-2)-4 = 0
    c. 7(x-6)+21 = 0
    d. 3(x+4)-9 = 0

25. There are two parallel lines x and y. One line s is passing through both these parallel lines such that <smx = 60°. What will be the value of angle x?

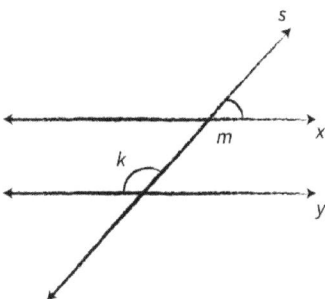

    a. 120°
    b. 60°
    c. 80°
    d. 150°

26. What will be the product of $3p^3-2p^2+p$ and $-2p$ will give?
    a. $-6p^4+4p^3-2p^2$
    b. $6p^4-4p^3+2p^2$
    c. $-6p^3+4p^2-2p$
    d. $6p^4+4p^3-2p^2$

27. We have two numbers x and y such that x+y=15, x-y=3. What will be the numbers?
    a. x=8, y=5
    b. x=10, y=7
    c. x=8, y=7
    d. x=9, y=6

28. $\frac{4}{5} \div \frac{6}{7} \times \frac{1}{2} + \frac{3}{2}$

   a. $\frac{56}{30}$
   b. $\frac{57}{30}$
   c. $\frac{58}{30}$
   d. $\frac{59}{30}$

29. What will be the value of $x^3+6x^2+12x+16$ when x = -2 ?

   a. 8
   b. 24
   c. 48
   d. 72

30. ABCD is a rectangle and inside it ABE is an Equilateral Triangle. What will be the angle <CEA represented by x in the figure?

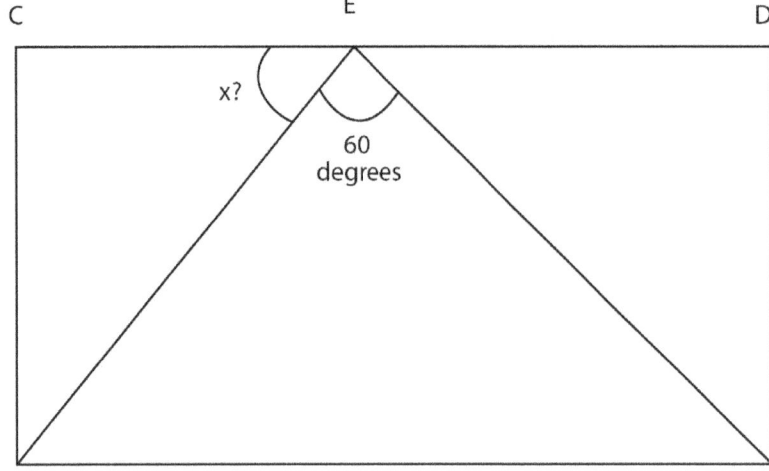

   a. 45°
   b. 50°
   c. 60°
   d. 55°

# MECHANICAL COMPREHENSION

1. P is a block of mass 5kg. At point Q, a block of mass 3kg was attached just to slide the block P.

   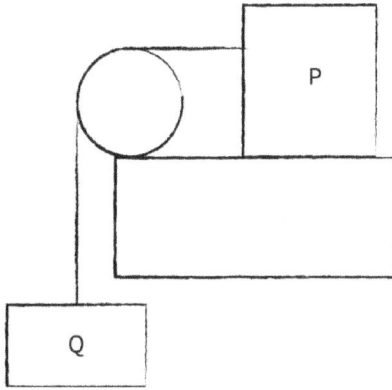

   If no displacement occurs, the coefficient of friction between the block P and the horizontal surface is:
   a. 0.5
   b. 0.6
   c. 0.7
   d. 0.8

2. A ball is thrown into the air. After few seconds, it returns back to the earth. What can be its likely cause?
   a. Earth's gravitational field pulls it back
   b. It's speed did not match the escape velocity of earth
   c. Neither of these is correct
   d. Both (a) and (b) are correct

3. The factor which distinguishes between a scalar and a vector quantity is:
   a. Magnitude
   b. Direction
   c. Both (a) & (b)
   d. Neither (a) nor (b)

4. An athlete couldn't stop himself immediately after crossing the finish line. He was explained why this was happening by Newton's:
   a. 1st law of motion
   b. 2nd law of motion
   c. 3rd law of motion
   d. Law of Universal Gravitation

5. How is the weight of a person in an elevator affected if the elevator accelerates upwards, accelerates downwards and is at rest?
    a. Increases, Decreases, Remains Constant
    b. Decreases, Remains Constant, Increases
    c. Remains Constant, Increases, Decreases
    d. Decreases, Increases, Remains Constant

6. In the above example of a lift, which of Newton's law is demonstrated?
    a. 1st law of motion
    b. 2nd law of motion
    c. 3rd law of motion
    d. Law of Universal Gravitation

7. The threads of a screw work on the principle of another type of simple machine, which is:
    a. Lever
    b. Inclined plane
    c. Wedge
    d. None of the above

8. The shaft of the screw penetrates wood through the principle of yet another simple machine, which is:
    a. Inclined plane
    b. Lever
    c. Wedge
    d. None of the above

9. The following objects are an example of which order of the lever:
    Forceps, Scissors, Fishing Rod, Bottle Opener
    a. 3rd, 2nd, 3rd, 1st
    b. 2nd, 3rd, 1st, 3rd
    c. 3rd, 1st, 3rd, 2nd
    d. 1st, 3rd, 2nd, 3rd

10. A mechanic observes that he is able to lift the car by 2cm if he moves the lever down by 30cm. if he is applying a force of 20N to the lever, the force applied by the lever on the car is:
    a. 250N
    b. 300N
    c. 350N
    d. 400N

11. Angular momentum of a body doesn't change if:
    a. External torque is not applied
    b. External torque is applied in CW Direction
    c. External torque is applied in CCW Direction
    d. External torque has no effect on the angular momentum of the body

12. Two moving bodies A & B possess the same amount of kinetic energy (see figure).

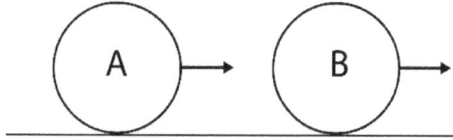

   If both the bodies are of unit mass then,
    a. Velocity of body A > Velocity of body B
    b. Velocity of body A = Velocity of body B
    c. Velocity of body A < Velocity of body B
    d. Cannot be determined, insufficient data

13. A flywheel, initially at rest, attains an angular velocity of 600rad/s in 15sec. Assuming constant angular acceleration, the angular displacement and angular acceleration of the flywheel in this time is:
    a. 4500rad, 40rad/s$^2$
    b. 5400rad, 40rad/s$^2$
    c. 4000rad, 45rad/s$^2$
    d. 4000rad, 54rad/s$^2$

14. The wedge angle of a particular wedge is increased. The Mechanical Advantage of the wedge:
    a. Increased
    b. Decreased
    c. Remained constant
    d. Any of the possibilities is likely as M.A. is not affected by the wedge angle

15. Calculate the Mechanical Advantage of the following wedge:

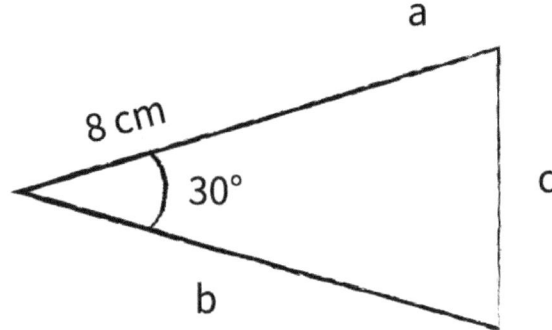

a. 1
b. 2
c. 3
d. 4

16. In the same question, the velocity of block Q, when it reaches a height of 7m above the ground is:
    a. 7.33m/s
    b. 7.66m/s
    c. 7.99m/s
    d. Cannot be determined, insufficient data

17. Observe the following figure:

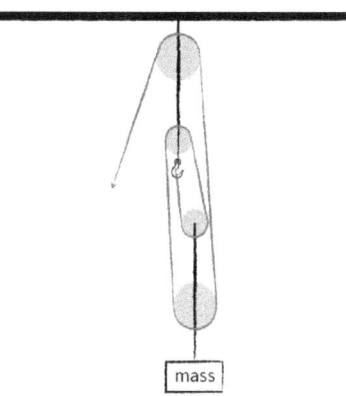

The mechanical advantage (IMA) for this frictionless pulley is:
a. 3
b. 4
c. 5
d. Insufficient data

18. A body even after applying a certain amount of force, did not move. What can be said about the frictional force acting on the body?
a. Less than µmg
b. More than µmg
c. Equal to mg
d. Equal to µmg

19. The gravitational force exerted by one object on another at macroscopic level:
a. Increases with the increase in distance
b. Decreases with the increase in distance
c. Remains constant
d. None of the above

20. The dimensional formula of Gravitational constant is:
a. $ML^2T^{-2}$
b. $M^{-1}L^3T^{-1}$
c. $M^{-2}L^2T^{-2}$
d. $M^{-1}L^3T^{-2}$

21. A fighter jet traveling at a speed of 630kmph drops a bomb 8secs before crossing over a target to accurately hit the target. How far was the jet from its target when it dropped the bomb?
    a. 1.2 km
    b. 1.4 km
    c. 1.6 km
    d. 1.8 km

22. Which of the following is not an equation of uniformly accelerated motion:
    a. $a = v^2-u^2/2s$
    b. $a = 2(s-ut)/t^2$
    c. $a = 2s-ut/t^2$
    d. $a = v-u/t$

23. Newton's 1st law of motion is based on the Galileo's law of inertia. Which of the following types of inertia satisfy this law:
    a. Inertia of Rest
    b. Inertia of Motion
    c. Inertia of Direction
    d. All of the above

24. Observe the figure below:

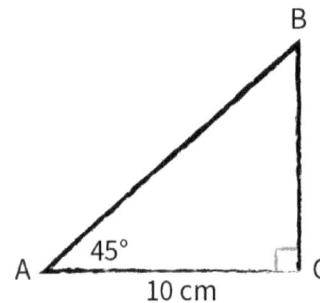

The Mechanical Advantage of the given ramp is:
a. 1.414
b. 0.141
c. 14.14
d. None of the above

25. Which of the following is not a part of the incline plane family of simple machines:
    a. Wedge
    b. Ramp
    c. Lever
    d. Screw

26. The mechanical advantage of a screw having 6 threads per inch and a radius of 0.1in is:
    a. 3.33
    b. 3.55
    c. 3.77
    d. 3.99

27. Effort is being put on a lever with a speed of 20cm/s at a distance of 2m from the fulcrum. The speed at which the load moves, if it is located at a distance of 50cm from the fulcrum is:
    a. 80 cm/s
    b. 100 cm/s
    c. 120 cm/s
    d. 140 cm/s

28. Calculate the amount of work done in moving a mass of 10kg at rest with a force of 5N in 8 seconds with no repulsive forces in action?
    a. 80J
    b. 100J
    c. 120J
    d. 60J

29. Consider 3 equal masses at arbitrary points A, B & C in space and let D be a point on the surface of the earth (as shown in the figure).

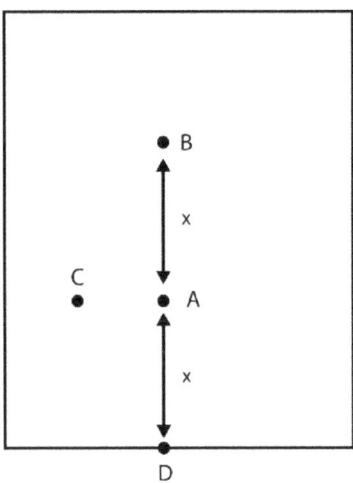

Then,
 i. The mass at point B has the maximum potential energy
 ii. Masses at points A & C have equal P.E. but less than that of the mass at point D
 iii. The mass at point D, if lifted to a height 2x, will possess P.E. equal to P.E(B).
   a. Statements (i), (ii) & (iii) are true
   b. Only statements (i) & (iii) are true
   c. None of them is true
   d. Only statements (i) is true

30. The disc in the figure is set to roll with angular velocity omega.

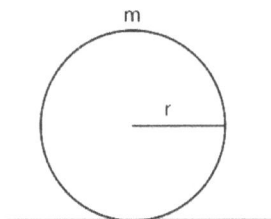

Total energy of the ball is:
   a. $1/2 \, mr^2 w^2$
   b. $3/4 \, mrw^2$
   c. $1/2 \, mrw^2$
   d. $3/4 \, mr^2 w^2$

6.1 – OAR Practice Test #2 Answer Key

## PARAGRAPH COMPREHENSION

1. A.
2. C.
3. C.
4. B.
5. A.
6. D.
7. B.
8. B.
9. A.
10. C.
11. D.
12. A.
13. B.
14. C.
15. B.
16. A.
17. D.
18. D.
19. B.
20. C.

# MATHEMATICS KNOWLEDGE

1. A.
2. B.
3. A.
4. D.
5. D.
6. A.
7. B.
8. D.
9. D.
10. C.
11. A.
12. C.
13. C.
14. D.
15. C.
16. A.
17. A.
18. B.
19. D.
20. C.
21. B.
22. A.
23. D.
24. C.
25. A.
26. A.
27. D.
28. D.
29. A.
30. C.

## MECHANICAL COMPREHENSION

1. B.
2. D.
3. B.
4. A.
5. A.
6. C.
7. B.
8. C.
9. C.
10. B.
11. A.
12. A.
13. B.
14. D.
15. B.
16. C.
17. A.
18. B.
19. D.
20. B.
21. C.
22. D.
23. A.
24. C.
25. C.
26. A.
27. A.
28. B.
29. D.
30. A.

# Exclusive Trivium Test Tips

Here at Trivium Test Prep, we strive to offer you the exemplary test tools that help you pass your exam the first time. This book includes an overview of important concepts, example questions throughout the text, and practice test questions. But we know that learning how to successfully take a test can be just as important as learning the content being tested. In addition to excelling on the [EXAM NAME], we want to give you the solutions you need to be successful every time you take a test. Our study strategies, preparation pointers, and test tips will help you succeed as you take the [EXAM NAME] and any test in the future!

## Study Strategies

1. Spread out your studying. By taking the time to study a little bit every day, you strengthen your understanding of the testing material, so it's easier to recall that information on the day of the test. Our study guides make this easy by breaking up the concepts into sections with example practice questions, so you can test your knowledge as you read.

2. Create a study calendar. The sections of our book make it easy to review and practice with example questions on a schedule. Decide to read a specific number of pages or complete a number of practice questions every day. Breaking up all of the information in this way can make studying less overwhelming and more manageable.

3. Set measurable goals and motivational rewards. Follow your study calendar and reward yourself for completing reading, example questions, and practice problems and tests. You could take yourself out after a productive week of studying or watch a favorite show after reading a chapter. Treating yourself to rewards is a great way to stay motivated.

4. Use your current knowledge to understand new, unfamiliar concepts. When you learn something new, think about how it relates to something you know really well. Making connections between new ideas and your existing understanding can simplify the learning process and make the new information easier to remember.

5. Make learning interesting! If one aspect of a topic is interesting to you, it can make an entire concept easier to remember. Stay engaged and think about how concepts covered on the exam can affect the things you're interested in. The sidebars throughout the text offer additional information that could make ideas easier to recall.

6. Find a study environment that works for you. For some people, absolute silence in a library results in the most effective study session, while others need the background noise of a coffee shop to fuel productive studying. There are many websites that generate white noise and recreate the sounds of different environments for studying. Figure out what distracts you and what engages you and plan accordingly.

7. Take practice tests in an environment that reflects the exam setting. While it's important to be as comfortable as possible when you study, practicing taking the test exactly as you'll take it on test day will make you more prepared for the actual exam. If your test starts on a Saturday morning, take your practice test on a Saturday morning. If you have access, try to find an empty classroom that has desks like the desks at testing center. The more closely you can mimic the testing center, the more prepared you'll feel on test day.
8. Study hard for the test in the days before the exam, but take it easy the night before and do something relaxing rather than studying and cramming. This will help decrease anxiety, allow you to get a better night's sleep, and be more mentally fresh during the big exam. Watch a light-hearted movie, read a favorite book, or take a walk, for example.

## Preparation Pointers

1. Preparation is key! Don't wait until the day of your exam to gather your pencils, calculator, identification materials, or admission tickets. Check the requirements of the exam as soon as possible. Some tests require materials that may take more time to obtain, such as a passport-style photo, so be sure that you have plenty of time to collect everything. The night before the exam, lay out everything you'll need, so it's all ready to go on test day! We recommend at least two forms of ID, your admission ticket or confirmation, pencils, a high protein, compact snack, bottled water, and any necessary medications. Some testing centers will require you to put all of your supplies in a clear plastic bag. If you're prepared, you will be less stressed the morning of, and less likely to forget anything important.
2. If you're taking a pencil-and-paper exam, test your erasers on paper. Some erasers leave big, dark stains on paper instead of rubbing out pencil marks. Make sure your erasers work for you and the pencils you plan to use.
3. Make sure you give yourself your usual amount of sleep, preferably at least 7 – 8 hours. You may find you need even more sleep. Pay attention to how much you sleep in the days before the exam, and how many hours it takes for you to feel refreshed. This will allow you to be as sharp as possible during the test and make fewer simple mistakes.
4. Make sure to make transportation arrangements ahead of time, and have a backup plan in case your ride falls through. You don't want to be stressing about how you're going to get to the testing center the morning of the exam.
5. Many testing locations keep their air conditioners on high. You want to remember to bring a sweater or jacket in case the test center is too cold, as you never know how hot or cold the testing location could be. Remember, while you can always adjust for heat by removing layers, if you're cold, you're cold.

Test Tips

1. Go with your gut when choosing an answer. Statistically, the answer that comes to mind first is often the right one. This is assuming you studied the material, of course, which we hope you have done if you've read through one of our books!
2. For true or false questions: if you genuinely don't know the answer, mark it true. In most tests, there are typically more true answers than false answers.
3. For multiple-choice questions, read ALL the answer choices before marking an answer, even if you think you know the answer when you come across it. You may find your original "right" answer isn't necessarily the best option.
4. Look for key words: in multiple choice exams, particularly those that require you to read through a text, the questions typically contain key words. These key words can help the test taker choose the correct answer or confuse you if you don't recognize them. Common keywords are: *most, during, after, initially,* and *first*. Be sure you identify them before you read the available answers. Identifying the key words makes a huge difference in your chances of passing the test.
5. Narrow answers down by using the process of elimination: after you understand the question, read each answer. If you don't know the answer right away, use the process of elimination to narrow down the answer choices. It is easy to identify at least one answer that isn't correct. Continue to narrow down the choices before choosing the answer you believe best fits the question. By following this process, you increase your chances of selecting the correct answer.
6. Don't worry if others finish before or after you. Go at your own pace, and focus on the test in front of you.
7. Relax. With our help, we know you'll be ready to conquer the [TEST NAME]. You've studied and worked hard!

Keep in mind that every individual takes tests differently, so strategies that might work for you may not work for someone else. You know yourself best and are the best person to determine which of these tips and strategies will benefit your studying and test taking. Best of luck as you study, test, and work toward your future!

# 7. Conclusion

*At Accepted, Inc. we strive to help you reach your goals. We hope this guide gave you the information to not only score well but to exceed any previous expectations. Our goal is to keep it concise, show you a few test tricks along the way, and to ultimately help you succeed in your goals. Please let us know if we've truly prepared you for the exam and if don't mind including your test score we'd be thankful for that too! Please send us an email to [feedback@acceptedinc.com](mailto:feedback@acceptedinc.com).*

*Remember – Study Smarter. Score Higher. Get Accepted!*

*-Accepted, Inc.-*